THE FIRE WITHIN

A True Story of Triumph Over Tragedy

VALERIE L. GREENE

Alex Press
Winter Park, Florida

ISBN 0-97488-338-7

Cover design by Debbie Billington /Art Sharks
Interior Design and Jacket Layout by Bookcovers.com
Author Photograph Color - Beverly Brosius
Author Photograph B/W - Dennis Dean Images

DEDICATION

In loving memory of my precious grandmother

and my faithful pet, Alex.

I miss you.

"It's in every one of us to be wise—

Find your heart,

Open up both your eyes.

We can all know everything without knowing why;

It's in every one of us by and by.

—Theme song from *The Experience*—

ACKNOWLEDGEMENTS

Thank you, God, for sparing my life and giving me a second chance to make a difference. May this book witness my willingness to listen to the message you put in my heart.

Thank you to all those who remembered me in your prayers.

I wish to thank all the rehab therapists and the nurses who cared for me and helped me to recover. Special thanks to my speech therapist, Terese Uliano for believing that one day I would become a inspirational speaker.

My deepest appreciation to Andy McGrane, Rhonna Bodin, Bill Spain, Bonnie Murdock, Edith Edwards, Eloise Engler, Karen Kulinich, Kevin and Kathleen Doll, Sandy Fink, Herb Hall, Randy Ellington, Meg Gaffney, Lori Lloyd, Lesley Lincoln, Helen and John Letter, Ena Serrano, Richard Smith, Mark Rash, Gary Sydnor, Anne Diebel, Mike Maher, Kelly Price, Mojka Renaud, Patricia Peters, Tom and Kathy Ferrante, Vivienne Bailey, Marie Wallaker, Tom Harmon, Donna Harris, Betsy Alaimo, Pat Crowe, Donna Eden, and Sandra Wand. Like angels that lift us to our feet, you have supported me, cared for me, laughed and cried with me, befriended me. You have become part of my journey of love and hope. Thank you for being there for me. Thank you for helping me to find my wings.

I would also like to thank those individuals who shared their time and talents, and helped me to birth this dream into reality. To Melody LeBaron, my life coach, thank you for bringing out all the difficult memories that were harbored in the chambers of my soul, for believing in my potential, and for teaching me how to hold a space of love and forgiveness. Jim Donovan, my book coach, thank you for your wonderful guidance and your get-it-done attitude. You're one Irishman I will always want in my corner!

Thank you to my dear sisters Angie and Michelle who love me no matter what. And, to their dear children Donnie, Alissa, Trevor, Victoria, and Trenton: I love you all very much!

And, to my mother and father, thank you for loving me and giving me the tools of survival—faith and humor. I love you!

CONTENTS

Introduction

This is a remarkable survival story about how a young woman overcame a devastating tragedy with amazing courage and faith.

The first time I met Valerie, I was struck by her ready, brilliant smile and her natural beauty that shone through the confusion and pain that had been thrust upon her. I was charmed by her undaunted spirit and quick wit in a situation that most would find overwhelming and absolutely humorless. Unlike those who knew Valerie before her stroke, I could not compare the "new" Valerie to the "old." All I knew was what I saw—a young woman who had survived a devastating injury that had crippled her and left her speechless, ripping out from under her a bright future as a highly successful financial consultant.

Valerie humbly won't share all of the details of her recovery, so take it from a loving witness, her recovery is a modern-day miracle, a manifestation of what she believed was possible.

It has not been an easy road, indeed the physical and emotional challenges would have overwhelmed most people, but she took them on, one at a time. Courage and faith became the cornerstone to her recovery. Courage to do what is necessary, and faith to believe that everything happens for a reason. Valerie's story reflects the power that is always with us, even in our darkest hour.

May Valerie's story inspire, enlighten, and encourage you, as it has me and a multitude of others.

Patricia Peters, LMT

As Valerie's reflexologist, I have had the privilege of knowing her for many years. I have witnessed as she strengthened her mind, body, and spirit—transforming her life in the process. Although she has experienced many forms of loss, she is an amazing survivor, tried and purified by fire!

We all come through our personal experiences with our own unique perspectives. It's how we transcend those life-changing situations that will determine how we choose to exist. Valerie chose to overcome and rise above her challenges.

I feel blessed to know Valerie, and I am glad that God allowed our paths to cross. She inspires me to be true to my journey and to manifest my fire within. Her recovery is a reflection of the power of God that is available to all of us.

May your life be touched by her remarkable story.

Vivienne Bailey, Reflexologist

CHAPTER ONE

The Day My Life Changed Forever

Monday, June 10, 1996   9:30 p.m.

Grasping the metal guard rails of my hospital bed, I cried out begging for the dizziness to stop. Everything was spinning. Terrified, my body trembled in fear.

"I-I-I-I neeeeeeeed yyyoouuuuuu ttttooo callll...," I pleaded for help. I was desperately trying to ask the nurse to call a doctor I knew, but my words ran together. Instead, I motioned for paper and pen and wrote my request as my hand shook.

"Call Dr. Powers," I wrote.

Dr. Powers was a neurosurgeon I trusted. I knew he would know what to do. The nurse returned moments later to tell me that he was out of the country attending a medical conference.

My heart sank as my mind raced frantically. What is going to happen to me now, I thought? I would have been even more alarmed had I known that the neurologist on call was the same doctor who'd seen me last year—and misdiagnosed me with *multiple sclerosis.*

The nurse asked Linda, the friend who'd driven me to the emergency room, to step outside the curtained area near my bed. I could hear the nurse asking her if she knew what might be causing my problem.

"Do you know if Valerie has taken anything? What about her family medical history?"

Linda assured the nurse that my problem was not drug-induced. "I don't know about her family history. She owns her own business and plays golf. She's very healthy; except, last year she had an incident like this where she got real dizzy and sick. I believe that a doctor later told her she'd had a mild stroke," Linda informed.

I was lying on my side in the bed holding my head. Cold. Weak. In pain. Terrified. The dizziness was overwhelming. I couldn't explain it. . . to Linda. . . or to the nurses. Why aren't they treating me? This is an emergency! Why is it taking so long?

I knew this was very serious and that I might be having a stroke. Last fall Dr. Powers told me he disagreed with the diagnosis of *multiple sclerosis* and believed I had suffered a mild stroke. This time I was experiencing something far more intense and much worse than before. It felt like someone was switching my brain off and on at random—like deliberate torture.

Finally, the staff physicians ran some tests, including a *CT scan*. It was past midnight when the nurse returned, reporting that the scans were normal. Stunned, I heard the nurse tell Linda to take me home, and let me "sleep it off."

I realized that they thought I was drunk. Even in my fear and outrage, I saw it from their perspective: My youth, my slurred speech, and my stumbling to the bathroom had painted a picture for the ER nurses of a young woman who'd had too many martinis.

NO! It should be easy enough to determine an alcohol-induced stupor from a stroke, I reasoned. I knew if I went home I might die alone. I refused to leave, insisting on more tests. I was put on a waiting list and, considering the late hour, Linda, who had to be at work the next morning, needed to go home.

I wanted someone to be with me. . . I wanted my mother. For years we had a very tense relationship and were not on speaking terms. We lived less than 20 minutes from each other, but our only contact was her occasional disapproving letters. I love my mother. Unfortunately, her idea of how I should live and her beliefs are different from mine. The wounds went deep, and I wasn't sure I wanted to reopen them. Finally, I asked

Linda to call her. Deep down inside, I feared I was dying and I wanted my mother.

It was 2 a.m. when my mother and stepfather arrived. She immediately came to my side, kissed my forehead, and held my hand. It was comforting to see my mom.

By this time, I'd completely lost the ability to talk. I could think clearly, but my words would vanish in thin air as soon as they reached the tip of my tongue. When the nurse came in, she explained to my mother that something terribly frightening must have happened to me to cause me to lose my voice.

I was shocked that they didn't even consider that I couldn't speak because I might be having a stroke! Had the thought even crossed their mind? I wrote a note to the nurse, asking her why an *MRI* had not been ordered. I knew that *MRIs* were more precise than *CT scans*.

In a matter-of-fact manner, she responded "Oh, the *MRI* machine is down for repairs. I'm going to give you a shot that will help you sleep. Now just get some rest, sweetie."

As I saw the needle coming, I realized that whatever she was injecting would mask my symptoms and numb my body's ability to respond to what was happening. All I could think was "If I'm having a stroke, this is going to kill me! You're going to kill me!"

The nurse left after assuring my mother again that they were doing all they could for me.

Several hours after I entered the hospital, I was finally moved out of the ER and into a room. Feeling my strength

deteriorate, I lay on the bed in a fetal position, vomiting—
then dry heaving—nonstop until I passed out.

Tuesday, June 11, 1996, 10 a.m.

I woke, surprised to still be alive, as I listened to a
nurse reassure my mother that a neurologist had been
called. Extremely thirsty, I wrote that I wanted water, but
was told I could have nothing to drink. Instead, the nurse
gave me another injection to control the nausea so I could
rest until the doctor arrived.

The day passed, and the neurologist never came.
Instead an intern examined me and told me just to rest.

That evening when my mom's best friend Edith, a
woman who is like an aunt to me, arrived, I felt relief.
Edith was sharp as a tack; maybe she would see that I
wasn't getting the help I needed. She took one look at me,
frozen in the fetal position, drooling, unable to speak, and
said, "Oh, dear God! Frances, she's dying! She's dying!"

She leaned over me, grabbed my hand, and said,
"Valerie, squeeze my hand if you can hear me."

I squeezed.

Rather than run for the nurses, Edith recognized what I
couldn't: The only one who could help me now was God.

"Frances, get on your knees!" Edith ordered. "We've got
to pray for your daughter; she's dying. We've got to pray!"

Edith and my mother both knelt beside my bed, praying
that God would spare my life. As I faded into unconsciousness,
I scribbled what I thought to be my last words:

As I Dying

My breathing slowed. The constant beeps of the machines and the voices of my mother and Edith faded into a velvety stillness. The edges of the room blurred as my eyes closed. As pain subsided and tension released, I knew my body was shutting down, yet I felt no fear. I felt safe and warm, as if I were being cradled in a womb.

Peace enveloped me, flooded through me. I was dying and was not afraid. As this tranquillity moved through me, I was surrounded by a bright whiteness. I knew this light—I had heard of it throughout my life. This was the presence of God. As my body lay limp on the bed, I experienced being lifted and carried like a wounded animal. I had always believed in God, but now I *knew* I was with God.

As I gave myself over to this peace, highlights of my life flashed before me, like a movie on fast-forward, slowing down to frame certain happy events: 5 years old, dressed in a fringed cowgirl miniskirt with a holster and guns; 7 years old, laughing with my sisters as we peeked out of our playhouse window; racing my dad to the lake for our annual swim contest the summer I was 16; crossing the finish line as I ran track in high school.

I saw less-happy times, as well: looking for—and not finding—my dad's shaving kit after my mother said he was gone; holding my cat while she died; being beat up on my first day of public school, entering sixth grade. Watching these times now, I felt no pain, only a peaceful acceptance.

And then I saw a funeral. My mother and dad weeping. My sisters sobbing. A multitude of friends covering the grounds of the cemetery. I realized that this was my funeral, that my family was weeping for me. Their grief stirred something in me, something that knew it was not my time to die. I shouted "NO!" and I suddenly jolted out of the white light, as if coming up out of the water, gasping for air.

"Lie still!" a voice commanded, as something sharp jabbed my right arm. I must have jerked as I came back into my body, just as the nurse was trying to insert an IV needle. She missed the vein, and it stung. Not fully aware, my instincts told my left hand to cover the sting—but my left hand, my left arm, was immobile. Paralyzed.

Awake now, I struggled to move—and found myself unable. Terrified, my brain reeled with questions. What is wrong? Why can't I move my arm and leg? What is going on? As I lost consciousness again, I prayed. Dear God, please help me!

The next thing I remember is hearing my older sister Angie and a man arguing in the hallway. Thirty-six hours after he was first called, the neurologist, Dr. Gonzalez, had finally arrived. I could hear Angie insisting that I was having a stroke.

Sounding exasperated, he responded emphatically, "There is no way this girl is having a stroke. She's too young!"

But Angie wouldn't back down. "How do you know it's not a stroke? How can you be sure? Given her history, you have to rule out all possibility of stroke!"

"To rule out all possibility of stroke, I would have to do an angiogram," Dr. Gonzalez replied.

"Do it! Do it now!" said Angie urgently.

As my gurney was being rushed through the hallway, Angie was running alongside, holding my hand. My friend Andy was on the other side, holding my other hand. As we paused at the doorway of the surgical area, Angie whispered words of encouragement and love.

"I'll see you soon," Angie said, as the nurse wheeled my gurney through the door. After the double doors swung shut, I heard her sobbing.

The room looked like an auto repair shop with different-sized tubes and hoses hanging from the wall. As I was placed on a cold metal table, a man wearing what looked like a welder's helmet, with a glass shield covering his face, told me that a small catheter would be inserted into the main artery through my thigh. A fluid dye would be injected that would show any blockages. He also explained the very real risk that if the needle punctured my artery, I might die during the procedure. I signed the papers, allowing them to proceed.

I could not be put under anesthesia for fear I would not come out of it. A shot numbed my leg. I watched on the monitor as a small tube was inserted into my right thigh, and the dye injected. The dye showed up on the monitor as a white line, traveling slowly up through my artery.

Hours later, I opened my eyes, feeling Angie's hand holding mine, hearing her voice telling me to hold on and fight. I was in the Critical Care Unit, lying in a bed covered with sheets, my right leg bandaged to protect the wound made by the incision. As the local anesthetic wore off, my leg

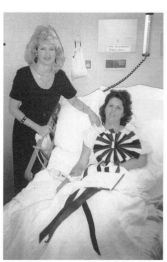

Valerie and Angie

felt like it was burning, pain radiating upward. Angie handed me a cup of water, but I was too weak to hold it to my lips. Her words of encouragement were comforting, but I could feel her fear.

When Dr. Gonzalez came into the room to give us the results of the tests, the look on his face said it all. I knew something was terribly wrong. He began explaining the results of the angiogram to my mother and sister and drew a diagram to show what had happened.

The test results were conclusive. I had suffered a massive stroke. A large blood clot had totally occluded the most vital artery in my brain stem. As a result, my entire left side was paralyzed leaving me unable to walk or talk.

Chapter Two

Surviving All Odds

> Looking back, with the clarity that comes from hindsight, I see now that my massive stroke was part of a process that began eight months earlier.

September 16, 1995

I'd come home from my office with a strange headache. I thought a shower would help me feel better, and then I'd lie down and rest before going to the Orlando Chamber networking event. I stepped into the shower, intending that the water flowing over my body would revive me.

Suddenly, I was in weightless motion, like an astronaut in space. I didn't know which way was up, down, or sideways. My equilibrium gone, I was falling, head over heels. . . over and over.

Knees buckling, I groped for the shower walls in an attempt to steady myself, surprised I was still upright. The motion continued and then—nausea and dizziness overwhelmed me. With great effort, I opened the shower door, grabbed the towel rack, and pulled myself out of the shower. As I sank to the floor, I saw my portable phone on top on the commode. I grabbed it and dialed 9-1-1. As the operator answered, I fell to the floor.

The sound of the paramedics breaking in the front door roused me.

"Dizzy. . . I'm so dizzy," I kept repeating.

My roommate Carol arrived home as the paramedics were carrying me out on a stretcher. I could see the concern on her face, but I knew she had a fear of hospitals.

I remember little of the ambulance ride. The vomiting began shortly after I arrived in the ER. As the nurse began questioning me, Carol's friend Tamara entered. I knew Carol had called her.

"What's wrong, Val?" she asked. "What happened?"

"I don't know. I was in the shower . . . I am just so dizzy."

Over the next few hours, as an *MRI* and other tests were done, my vomiting turned into dry heaving. Tamara had to look away as my body jerked with convulsions. I asked her to get me water, but the nurses would not allow me to have any. Finally, the results of the tests were in, and a neurologist was consulted. The diagnosis was: migrainous in origin.

Tired and weak, I could finally go home. The internist who was selected from my insurance plan wrote me a prescription for *Inderal* and told me to see her in two weeks.

October 1995

Two weeks later, I sat in her office as she quickly glanced through my file. She sighed as she looked at my *MRI* results.

"Your *MRI* appears irregular. But these readings are so sensitive it's probably only a false positive. You don't want this on your medical records, not at your age. It would be hard to get insurance." Never telling me exactly what she saw on the *MRI*, she told me to keep taking the *Inderal*.

As I walked down the hall after leaving her office, I glanced up and saw the name of a young doctor I'd been seeing on a professional basis, Gregg M. Powers, M.D. I knew him to be one of Orlando's leading neurosurgeons. Standing in front of his door, I hesitated, and then—as if a hand on my back propelled me—I opened the door and walked in. Without planning to, I asked the receptionist if Dr. Powers was in. To my surprise, a few moments later, he came to the lobby.

"Val! Good to see you! What brings you in?" he asked.

As we walked back to his office, I explained what had happened. After he'd examined me, he recommended that I redo the *MRI*.

Although I respected Dr. Power's advice and had agreed to another *MRI,* I was in no hurry to rush back to have the claustrophobic and time-consuming procedure repeated. Over the next few days, I continued to go into my office and see my scheduled clients. After one appointment, I told my business partner Eric that I felt extremely tired and lethargic.

"Val, if you feel that bad, just go home and rest," he said.

When I arrived home early that October evening I went straight to bed. In the middle of the night, I was awakened by a severe headache and a piercing pain that was isolated on the right side of my face, particularly my jaw. The pain was so intense I felt like my teeth were going to pop out. Never having had a migraine before, I assumed this pain was what my friends who did suffer with migraines complained about. I learned later that although a stroke itself is not painful, the symptoms leading up to it are bizarre and often excruciating.

If only I had known then what I know now: that stroke can happen to any of us—even healthy young women, that my body was exhibiting several of the warning signs of stroke, that I needed to get myself to a hospital and receive medical treatment. Instead, I took another *Inderal* and fell asleep.

By morning, I was too weak to move. The right side of my body felt heavier than my left. An irritating buzzing in my ears remained constant. Whatever had hit me was hard and fast. It took weeks before I was strong enough to walk around. I slowly weaned myself off the *Inderal* as I suspected this may have been contributing to my weakness.

November 1995

Within a couple of months I was better. Although my right side was still weaker than my left, I was mobile and ready to put this behind me. To look at me, no one would ever imagine I had suffered a stroke. Not even me. Why would that even be considered? I was only 31 years old. I ran into Dr. Powers, and he was concerned when I described what had happened. As a neurosurgeon, he could not treat me, because I didn't need surgery. But he offered to call the neurologist who had reviewed my hospital tests and suggest that more tests be done. He also requested that I have an *MRI* film sent to him, as he was now very curious about what was going on.

"Gregg, you know I hate that closed-*MRI* machine," I complained. "It's frightening to be in that dark thing—it feels like a casket."

"OK, then go to Duran Medical Clinic and get it done on their new open-*MRI* machine. The results won't be quite as detailed as films from a closed-*MRI*, but at least it will show me the basic picture."

Within a week, I had the *MRI* done at Duran Medical

and had been admitted to the hospital for tests. After the tests were complete, I waited patiently, lying in the hospital bed. I could hear Dr. Powers and another doctor arguing right outside my door. The new *MRIs* showed that I now had a lesion on my brain that was not there on the previous films. The other doctor insisted that the lesion was a result of *multiple sclerosis*. Dr. Powers argued that the lesion was caused by a stroke, due to the sudden onset.

Dr. Powers politely left to continue his rounds. The door to my room opened and a short, dark haired man with a mustache walked over to my bed.

"Hi, I'm Dr. Gonzalez," he said as he shook my hand. He turned and grabbed the side chair, swung it around backwards, and straddled it. Resting his arm on the back of the chair, while holding his clipboard, he began to explain.

"Ms. Greene, I have reviewed your latest test results. While there is a difference of opinion between myself and your friend Dr. Powers, as your neurologist, I am concluding that what you are suffering from is *multiple sclerosis.*"

As he began describing what that meant, I burst into tears. He waited a moment and began to explain that *multiple sclerosis* is aggravated by tension and stress. He strongly advised me to take some time off work.

While this diagnosis was naturally upsetting to me, I couldn't help but wonder if Dr. Powers had been right. After I returned home, I pulled out one of my medical books and began comparing stroke to *multiple sclerosis* (MS). My career training included insurance underwriting, so I had the resources to satisfy my curiosity about this diagnosis. Stroke and MS do have similar symptoms, however the distinction between the two is in the onset. MS is a progressive disease which slowly deteriorates the myelin sheath around the nerves. Stroke, as the name implies, hits suddenly. After reading this, I agreed with Dr. Powers, that my lesion was a result of a stroke.

Winter 1996

But I took Dr. Gonzalez's advice to take it easy. Allowing Eric, my business partner, to take over our shared work, I went to Pensacola to spend a few months recuperating. My sister Angie, her husband Don, and 7-year-old son Donnie offered to let me stay with them until I could return to work.

Pensacola borders the Gulf of Mexico and is a charming, historical town with breathtaking views. Famous for its snowy white beaches and crystal-clear, aqua-green water, it has been named the Emerald Coast. Pensacolians are proud of the fact that it is a quiet place to raise a family—but the pace in this small town was much too slow for me. Now I could see why Angie considered me a "city slicker."

Back home, I woke at the crack of dawn, worked out at the gym, and was on my way to the office by 8 a.m. My evenings had been filled with meetings and social events. Angie's temperament and schedule were very different from mine. She came to life very slowly in the mornings, as she fixed breakfast, packed Donnie's lunch, and drove him to school. In the evenings, we ate dinner around the dining room table, and then watched TV in the family room by the fireplace. To me, Angie's life felt like a rerun of *Leave It to Beaver.*

I continued to wake early, as usual, making a list of things to do. Before Angie had time to brush her teeth, I was knocking at her bedroom door, asking when we could go to the post office.

"Valerie, why on earth do you need to go to the post office? And why every day?"

"I need to mail out some important letters," I answered.

I was bored; she was frustrated. My so-called "relaxation" included gathering twigs for the evening fire and reading Angie's *Better Homes and Gardens* with my Persian cat Alex nestled in my lap.

One cold day, snuggled in front of the fire in Angie's big easy chair, I was skimming another magazine when an article on the "Top Ten Neurologists in the U.S." caught my attention. Glancing through it, I saw that one of them, Dr. Rockwell, was practicing at the University of South Alabama—less than an hour from my sister's house. When I showed the article to Bonnie, Angie's best friend, she insisted that I call his office. I knew he would not be easy to see. Nonetheless, I called and left a message with his staff requesting an appointment. The next day they called me back and explained that Dr. Rockwell would see me only after first reviewing my *MRI* films. So, I arranged for a copy of my films to be sent to him. When I got an appointment, I was thrilled!

Angie agreed to drive me to my appointment if we could stop afterwards and visit our friends the Jarrads in Mobile, Alabama. When Dr. Rockwell walked into his office and introduced himself to me and Angie, we looked at each other in surprise. I knew what she was thinking: "Could this tall, blonde, blue-eyed hunk of a man really be your doctor, Val?"

Yes, and a good one, too. First he looked at my medical information, then he did a basic neurological evaluation. He asked me to follow his index finger with my eyes, as he moved it from left to right in front of me. Then, he asked me to close my eyes, hold my arms out to the side, and with one hand at a time, touch the tip of my nose. He did a reflex test on my knees and ran a needle lightly across the soles of my feet.

After this examination, he sat on the wheeled stool next to the table I was sitting on. He confidently discarded the idea that I had MS and explained why he was convinced that I'd had a stroke. He recommended I begin aquatic therapy to strengthen my weak side and continue taking aspirin.

By the end of May, I felt well enough to return home. My friend Andy helped me load my stuff in a U-Haul and drove me and my cat Alex back to Winter Park. I'd been

looking forward to getting back to the office. But now I
felt tired and weak, like I had a touch of the flu. Since I
hadn't been home long, I didn't have any food in the
house. I called my grandmother who lived nearby and
asked her if she could bring me some dinner. Throughout
my childhood, my mother's mother had always been there
for me; she loved to cook and she was well known for her
comforting Southern meals. Soon, she and my
grandfather were walking up the front walkway, my
grandmother carrying a basket filled with food. As she
entered the house, the comforting aroma of pot roast,
potatoes, and warm rolls filled the den. And, of course,
there was something sweet for later.

In her familiar caring manner, she propped me up on
the sofa with pillows and brought me a plate of food.
After I'd eaten, she insisted that she was going to stay with
me. She kissed my grandfather goodnight and he went
home.

June 1, 1996

I was grateful that she had stayed as I grew worse
during the night. The next morning I woke up dizzy and
feeling nauseated. We called Eloise, a friend of the family,
to drive us to the hospital, which was only a couple of
minutes from the house. I wanted to be examined. I
wasn't taking any more chances with my health.
During the examination, my grandmother grilled the
doctor about his credentials, and after discovering that he

was single, she arched her eyebrow and looked at me pointedly. She'd never stopped hoping I'd marry a doctor. I was more concerned with explaining that I'd been to the hospital last fall with similar symptoms. "We're going to run some tests and find out what you've got," he said confidently. When he returned to the room, he seemed intent on touting his vast knowledge of the brain before he shared his diagnosis: *vertigo*—a condition that causes extreme dizziness. He sent me home with a prescription for *meclizine* to control the dizziness.

That weekend my sister Angie drove down from Pensacola and picked me up to visit some friends in Sarasota. The morning after we arrived, I spent all day on the sofa with a low fever. I wanted to be home in my own bed. But Angie was having a great time visiting and did not want to leave. So, the man of the house offered to drive me home so Angie could stay longer. On the way home, I called a friend and asked if she would be kind enough to meet me at my house, as I didn't feel well.

Monday, June 10, 1996, 9 p.m.

Arriving home I walked through the front door where I immediately dropped my pillow on the cool wood floor and curled up, nauseated and too sick to move. My friend Linda arrived just minutes later. She helped me to the sofa and fixed me a bowl of soup. The warm food revived me a bit and we both felt relieved—until I started slurring my words. She quickly helped me out to the car and drove me to the hospital.

THREE

Critical Care

> The aftermath of a stroke is much like the calm after a storm. I lay in the Critical Care Unit, my body spent, as I drifted in and out of sleep, barely able to comprehend what had happened to me.

Thursday, June 13, 1996

"Is there anything else you would like?" Angie asked me. At that moment, weak with exhaustion and despair, all I wanted was comfort. Waves of hunger washed over me, and so did a memory of being out late with friends and stopping at Krystal for those tiny burgers and fries. Taking a pencil and pad of paper, I wrote down *"Krystal."*

Unsure at first, Angie finally understood what I wanted. She knew what I didn't realize—that I was not allowed to have food—but she left to go get what she thought might be my last request. I fell back to sleep.

"Val, wake up."

Someone was whispering my name. It was Angie. As I groggily opened my eyes, I felt something pressed up to my lips. What, I wondered, is that smell? A Krystal burger? Why on earth would she bring me a Krystal burger? She'd torn the small burger into tiny bites and, like a mother feeding an uncooperative baby, she was trying to entice me to eat before the nurses found out. Not remembering my earlier request, I turned my head away and fell back asleep.

"Be strong, Val." Angie was speaking again. "Be strong." I could feel the warmth of her love.

"Remember when we were kids and we played cowgirls and Indians? You were always the leader, Val. You were so brave. Pick up your gun. Fight. Please fight."

She was pressing something cold and hard into my right hand. I opened my eyes. It was a cap gun.

"Come on, Val," she was saying. "Remember what you were like then. Fight this. Be strong. You can do it."

I tried to grasp the gun, but it weighed as much as a bowling ball. Weakly, I pressed it back into Angie's hand, willing her to understand that I couldn't be strong now; I couldn't fight. I needed her to be the strong one.

Friday, June 14, 1996

The next day family and friends came to visit me. My

grandmother in her wide brimmed hat and my mother gathered around my bed, holding their hymnals, singing. Their slow hymns felt like funeral songs to me, so I wrote a note and handed it to my friend Dr. Spain, who had flown in from Pensacola. I felt sure he would understand, as he was very charismatic. He understood what I needed and said, "Come on now; let's sing something cheerful."

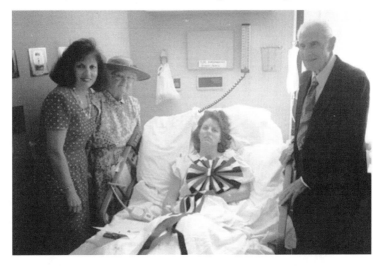

Val, Mom and Grandparents

Respectfully, they followed his lead and joined in his upbeat rendition of some lively hymns.

I asked about my father, who was living in Maine, and my younger sister Michelle, who lived in Maryland. Angie assured me that they had been called. She also said that Andy had spent the night at my house and would be in soon.

I'd met Andy after my mild stroke last fall. He had taken me to a doctor's appointment as a favor to one of our friends who couldn't. Right away, Andy and I just

clicked and became good friends. We would talk on the
phone often, and during his trips through North Florida,
he would stop and visit me while I was staying with Angie
in Pensacola.

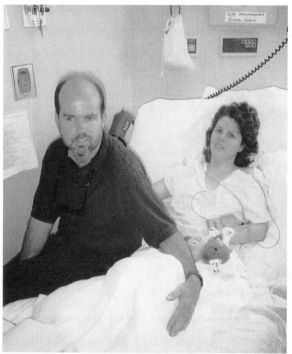

Valerie and Andy

When Andy arrived, he brought a wonderful surprise.
Knowing how much I loved my cat Alex, Andy brought
him to the hospital, sneaking him past security in a duffel
bag. He sat the bag on the bed and a little black head
popped out. It was Alex! I burst into tears of joy. My
furry companion laid on my chest and purred. He had
missed me, too.

Later that afternoon, tired and weak, still covered with wires and tubes, I finally nodded off to sleep. The nurses sent everyone home. Exhausted as I was, unfamiliar noises kept startling me awake. The rattling of food carts, machines beeping, the distant sounds of people talking. Monitoring my status throughout the night, the nurses woke me up several times.

"When am I ever going to get to sleep?" I wondered. I would doze off after their prodding and poking. Finally, toward morning, I fell into a deep sleep.

Saturday, June 15, 1996

At 5 a.m., on came the bright lights, startling me awake. It was the lab technician to draw blood. Blood drawings were difficult for me, as my veins were small and hard to find. After he left, I fell asleep again.

When I awakened, I was being transferred to a regular room. Finally! I was making progress. I was grateful to be unhooked from the loud monitors.

After I was settled in my new room, alone, I thought about what the doctor had told me. I just couldn't believe that I was paralyzed. Nonsense, I thought. This doctor has just screwed up again. The only way to know for sure was for me to find out on my own. To get out of bed and stand up. So I slowly scooted over to the edge of the bed—my entire left side still numb and lifeless. It wasn't easy, but I was determined to make it. I continued inching my way over to the edge, having no idea this maneuver required the use of balancing skills that I had lost.

Suddenly, I collapsed to the floor. My left side was like heavy jelly.

Reality sunk in.

I was *paralyzed.*

It wasn't until that moment that I fully comprehended the doctor's words that I may never walk again.

I was there several minutes, frightened, unable to move, before a nurse arrived and saw me on the floor.

"Oh my God, child, what have you done?" she asked.

I opened my mouth to explain, but nothing came out. She helped me get back in bed and called the doctor, who was doing rounds.

Minutes later, the doctor came in and began asking me questions.

"Do you know where you are?"

"Who is the President of the United States?"

"What year is it?"

"Why is he asking me these silly questions?" I wondered, as I easily wrote my answers. I later realized that he was trying to determine if I had fully lost my mental capacity. Fortunately, my mental faculties were intact; however, I struggled with comprehension and reasoning.

My friend Andy walked into the room, and the doctor asked if I knew who he was. I smiled and nodded my head and wrote the name "Elvis." The doctor looked shocked—afraid I was worse off than he'd thought. Andy laughingly explained that "Elvis" was a nickname I'd given him, because he once lived near Graceland. Thank God I still had my sense of humor.

The doctor proceeded with more questions and several reflex tests, running a needle lightly along my face and down the left side of my body to the bottom of my foot, asking if I felt anything. I watched in bewilderment, shocked that I felt no sensation. Then the doctor asked me to move my fingers and toes. No problem, I thought. I can do that! But . . . nothing. No movement. Oh, God, this can't be happening! Not to me. This felt like a scene from a movie, happening to someone else.

Before leaving, the doctor explained that the next step for me was rehabilitation. "In rehab, you will receive therapy for all this."

"How soon?" I wrote.

"As soon as your insurance approves it," the doctor replied. "We've already contacted your insurance carrier to let them know that rehab is needed. Unfortunately, approval can take several days."

As soon as the doctor left, I wrote a note to Andy, asking him to call my friend Herb, who handled my health insurance. I felt sure he could expedite my transfer.

I'd met Herb years ago, when he had joined the first investment and insurance firm I represented. Herb was a recent University of Central Florida graduate and a noted football player. Over 6 feet tall, he was a sharply dressed handsome black man, with an enthusiasm and work ethic that was very visible.

Being the two youngest reps in the all white male firm, Herb and I quickly connected and became friends. We laughingly referred to ourselves as the "token" duo—a black man and a woman.

Within a year of starting my own business, I encouraged Herb to do the same. With a giant leap of faith and a lot of work, he did just that. Over the years, his business grew into one of the most successful insurance agencies in the state of Florida.

I was relieved and comforted to know that my friend and powerful insurance agent would help me get transferred into rehab as soon as possible.

That afternoon, a group of friends came to cheer me up. Everyone took turns saying a few words of encouragement as they hung a large "Get Well" poster that they had all signed over my bed. I was grateful for their company, but I was also very embarrassed. Unable to hold my neck up, drooling, and the left side of my face drawn down and drooping, I was not a pretty sight. Normally very well groomed, I was now wearing an ugly hospital gown, my hair was a fright, and I wore no makeup. I reached up to my face to wipe the drool off the left side of my mouth. I looked pathetic. They tried to mask their fear and pity, but I could see it in their faces.

After they left, I began to think, "This can't be me! I've got to get out of here! I have to get into rehab and begin recovering so I can get back to work."

I wrote Andy another note: "Call Herb!"

"We already called him," Andy said.

"Call again!" I wrote.

The stroke had traumatized my nervous system so severely that the least little thing would set off intense frustration and exaggerate my already impatient nature. It had only been an hour since we'd called Herb. Even so, several times that day and the next, Andy willingly called Herb every time I asked to find out if Herb had made progress with the insurance company.

Sunday, June 16, 1996

Angie, Andy, and my mom were taking turns staying with me, and when I needed assistance from the nurses, they would press the CALL button. When the nurse responded "Yes?" over the intercom, they could tell the nurse what I needed. But at night, and sometimes during the day, I was alone. One time, I needed urgently to use the bathroom. I found the CALL button, pressed it with my good hand and waited.

A few seconds later, a voice responded "Yes?"

But I couldn't speak. I couldn't tell her what I needed. I tried to force air through my vocal cords and nothing would come out.

I pressed the CALL button again. But by the time the voice responded "Yes?" it was too late. I had wet the bed.

"Do you need something?" the voice asked.

Again I could not respond. I lay in wet sheets for quite a while until Andy arrived. Embarrassed, I wrote him a note explaining what had happened. He quickly called the nurses, and they came to change the bed linens and clean me.

After the nurse had changed the sheets, she put a plastic pad under me and said matter-of-factly, "If it happens again, feel free to wet the bed."

"NO!" I thought. "Do they have any idea what it feels like to be so helpless, so humiliated?"

She assured me that she'd tell all the nurses on the shift to respond in person when I pressed the CALL button.

"But if we're all busy and can't get here in time," she explained, "it will be easier for us to change this pad than to change the whole bed."

I had no choice but to let the plastic pad stay. This horrified me; it was so degrading. Little did I know that this indignity was the first of many. Lying in a urine-stained hospital bed, paralyzed, and totally dependent on others, I feared that my life would never be the same.

Tuesday, June 18, 1996

After what seemed like an eternity, a therapist from rehab came to my room with a wheelchair. "Ms. Greene, your insurance company has approved inpatient rehabilitation, and I'm here to take you to your new room in the rehab wing." Relieved, I thought, "Yes! You did it, Herb!"

Being wheeled down the corridors, I was excited to begin my recovery. I naively thought I would only be there a few days, and then I could go home! I had no idea that I'd be in the hospital for over a month!

When we arrived at my room, I stared at the room number, 1481. It was the same number as my home street address. How bizarre! My first reaction was that the nurses had done that on purpose to make me feel at home. Years later I realized it was one of those synchronistic coincidences that let us know we are on our path.

It was late afternoon when I was transferred, and after the nurse had settled me in my bed, I surveyed my room. There was a big window with a view of the grounds leading to the parking lot—but the way my bed faced, all I could see was the side of a brick wall. In addition to the bed, nightstand, and dresser, on the white walls hung a TV, a clock, a calendar, and a bulletin board listing my therapy schedule.

Not the best design to cheer a person up. It felt like a prison cell, although I'm sure it was more lavish than that. Wishing I had some of my photography to hang on the walls, I watched the large clock tick, counting the minutes. Each minute felt like an hour.

It was June 18th. Looking at the calendar on the wall I thought of my daily planner at work, remembering how full the pages were with long lists of tasks to do and clients to call. Would I ever return to work? What about driving?

Oh my God, I hadn't thought about driving. I love driving. Would I ever drive again? As my mind raced, I became overwhelmed with anxiety.

June 19 through June 30, 1996

The next afternoon, my mother arrived with a plate of warm food. I didn't care for the hospital food—except for their fresh-baked chocolate chip cookies, so having her home-cooked meals was a wonderful treat.

She would take my laundry home each day, as she knew how I loved to have my things clean and in order. One day, during my free time, she drove me to see our friend Mojka, who is an acupuncturist and homeopathic physician. My mother felt certain Mojka could help me, and she was right. Mojka started me on homeopathic remedies, nutritional supplements, and acupuncture treatments, all of which produced remarkable results.

After several sessions with Mojka, my mother thought that my comprehension had returned. Unfortunately, this was a process that would take years.

The next time she came to visit me, I sensed something different about her. I noticed that in addition to her Bible, she also carried several booklets and tapes. Oh no, I thought. Here it comes. She's going to preach.

She chatted with the nurse, who was taking my vital signs. But I could feel the familiar tension rising. As soon as the nurse left the room, she began.

"Valerie, I am worried about you. You are living outside the will of God. You must repent and turn back to Him."

Without the power of speech, I could only listen.

"Valerie, I'm only saying this because I love you! God

will not be mocked! You must repent. If you want me in your life, if you want me to help you, you MUST renounce your lifestyle and return to Him!" She opened her Bible and began quoting scriptures.

We had been through this before, and I had stopped trying to explain myself to her. In the past, I would just get up and leave. But now I lay in bed—unable to move—as she recited the familiar scriptures and insisted I change.

"If you will not make that commitment, Valerie, then I have no other choice but to leave and not return until you do."

I closed my eyes, weeping silently, while she left. The familiar pain of rejection pierced my heart. Once again, I would be shut out of her life.

When Angie and Andy arrived, they tried to comfort me. They reassured me that I would be OK and that they would never leave me. They understood the innocent, childlike fear, common to stroke victims, that I was feeling. They understood my need for love and reassurance. Andy shared with me that he'd tried to talk to my mother. The conversation was filled with scriptures and my mother's fearful judgments of what would happen to me after I die; Andy wasn't able to get a word in edgewise. But he did leave with some insight.

"Your mother does love you," Andy gently explained. "But her fears for you are overwhelming. She is intensely devoted to her belief system, and I can understand why. Her church was her only safe haven when her world fell apart. Those people, that dogma, that interpretation of

scripture—it all gave her a sense of herself, defined who
she is and how the world works. Everything is either black
or white, sharply defined. If you live in accordance with
her 'convictions,' she considers you safely 'in the will of
God.' If you live outside her version of God's law, there is
only one way she can see you—as unrighteous."

"But I'm her *daughter!* Why can't she just love me
unconditionally? Why can't she just accept me?" I wrote,
still crying.

"She has been taught to interpret parts of the Bible
with harsh exactness," Andy said sadly. "While
disregarding Christ's commandment not to judge others."

That night, in the dark silence, my loneliness was
unbearable. As I lay on my side in the fetal position, my
mother's judgment and rejection came flooding back to
me, and I began sobbing. One of the night nurses heard
me and came in the room. I don't know if someone had
told the nurses about my mother leaving, but somehow
this angel of a nurse knew that I needed comforting. She
sat on the edge of my bed and rubbed my back with baby
powder until I fell fast asleep.

When I awoke in the morning, I had to use the
bathroom. I pressed the CALL button and waited. Once
again, I tried to say something, but nothing came out.

When I realized no one was coming, I decided to crawl
to the bathroom. But in sliding off the bed, I fell and cut
my face on the bedside table. Hearing the crash, the
nurses came running. When Angie arrived at lunch to

take me out, I was sitting on the edge of the bed, my face bandaged. She was livid—and filed a complaint. After that, the nurses responded in person.

The nurses seemed even more attentive after watching a recorded TV spot about me. It was aired in Pensacola by my friend Dr. Spain, who hosted a TV show on health. During a broadcast, he showed a photo of me with Angie, described my stroke, and asked his viewers to pray for me and send cards to my room. Angie brought a videotape of the show, reserved the rehab VCR, and invited several of my nurses to watch it with us.

As the photo of me came on the TV, I cried, remembering how attractive and strong I used to feel. That beautiful businesswoman looked so confident and proud. Now I felt like a monster. The nurses were saying, "Wow! Look at how pretty you are!" I knew their intentions were

Val and Angie

good, but it was the kind of praise you would give to a young child. I was insulted. I was unable to see that in many ways, I had become like a little child.

CHAPTER FOUR

Starting Over

> I was in the hospital for over a month.
> Each day I focused on only one thing:
>
> going home!

My life was humbled. Overnight I had gone from being a well-spoken entrepreneur to making garbled sounds and having to be taken to the restroom. I went from being totally independent to being totally dependent. My attitude, sense of humor, and faith in God were vital to my survival. Deep within I believed that in time I would understand the reason why I had been chosen to endure this experience. For now I had to survive.

Awakened by bright lights at 5:30 a.m., I kept my eyes closed as a lab technician once again drew blood from my arm. I was on a blood thinner, *Coumadin*, that had to be monitored. After a week of daily draws, my arm was so bruised it turned black and blue from my hand to my elbow. This bothered Angie and hurt me, so she insisted they draw blood only three times a week. What a relief it was when my doctors later changed my medication to *Plavix*, which didn't require so much monitoring and didn't leave me feeling lethargic and weak.

I requested to be given a shower every morning. Fortunately, my hygiene habits were still intact. The experience of being showered was humiliating—and, at first, frightening. At 6 a.m., a nurse wheeled me down the hall into a large tiled area, moved me onto a plastic chair that had a hollow seat, and helped me undress. As I sat naked and shivering, waiting for the shower to come on, a scrambled memory of a holocaust documentary flashed through my mind and sent fear through my body. My memories were scrambled, and I was afraid. After being toweled dry, I was wheeled back to my room and dressed.

Later that day, when Angie arrived, I wrote her a note, "They are trying to kill me."

"What?"

"In the showers," I wrote. "They are trying to kill me. They are Nazis."

"What on earth do you mean?" she asked.

"They are trying to gas me in the showers."

Disturbed, Angie walked down to the nurse's station and asked to see where I was showered. I could hear her walking back toward my room with a nurse. As they stood outside my door, I heard them talking.

"After a stroke," the nurse was saying, "many patients' memories are stirred up. Imagine a file cabinet that was ransacked—all the file folders and papers are scattered on the floor. The information you need is all there, but it cannot be easily retrieved. Hopefully, your sister will be able to reorganize all those files, but it will take time."

When Angie returned, she reassured me that she had checked the showers carefully and they were fine. I wrote, begging her to take me home for my showers, but she knew she couldn't, so she tried her best to calm my fears.

After about a week of daily showers, that fear went away, as my brain and nervous system began settling down. However, fear and frustration were my constant companions.

Challenges consumed my every effort; even using the bathroom was work. Once I was finally able to use the restroom rather than a bedpan, a nurse would have to assist me to sit on the toilet. My leg and trunk muscles were so weak, I had to hold onto the nurse as she lowered me slowly onto the toilet. Before she left, she made sure I knew to pull the red "Help" cord hanging from the wall so she would know when to come lift me up.

Simple tasks, like brushing my teeth and tying my tennis shoes for rehab, were tedious and time-consuming. Doing everything with one hand might seem easy—until you have no other choice. And fixing my hair—well, that's another story. Most of the time, I wore a baseball cap to cover my bad hair days. Thank God there wasn't a mirror in my room. I'd glimpsed my drooping face in the bathroom mirror, and it was scary.

Presenting myself well had always been important to me. My grandmother taught me early that our appearance is one of the few ways we have to represent ourselves. Upon entering the business world, I became even more discerning about my appearance—dressing for success.

My wardrobe included several lounging outfits to wear around the house. They were perfect for rehab. As soon as I was able to wear my own clothes, Angie brought these comfortable outfits, neatly arranging the pants and the coordinating tops in the dresser. The nurses who dressed me on my first few days in rehab must have been too busy to notice that certain tops went with certain pants. It bothered me to mismatch them. When Angie arrived, I wrote her a note asking her to help me change my clothes.

She read my note and asked, "What's wrong with what you are wearing? You look fine."

"Can't you see they don't match?" I wrote, frustrated.

I pointed to the pattern on my sleeve that didn't match my pants. She had to look twice before she noticed the black striped pattern down the side of sleeves.

"Oh, good grief, Val!" Angie exclaimed. "Are you referring to the design? It's hardly noticeable! But I'll change you if that will make you happy!"

One of my rehab nurses stopped in just after she'd helped me put on the correct pants. Angie asked her if they could chat in the hallway. I listened closely to hear their conversation.

"Since the stroke, she has the strangest fears—and she gets so frustrated about the smallest things," Angie said.

"That is totally normal," the nurse assured her. "Valerie's brain—her whole body—has been traumatized by the stroke. She is one of the lucky ones: Her memory and cognitive functions are returning, but everything is still scrambled and finding its way. This extreme sensitivity is perfectly normal at this stage. And because Valerie cannot tell us what she needs, she is incredibly frustrated. So don't worry; she'll be fine. Just give her some time."

When Angie came back in the room, she seemed relieved.

From then on, the nurses made sure that my clothes coordinated. It wasn't long before I came to think of my nurses as angels. They watched over me and cared for me with great compassion.

After my early-morning shower and the challenges of getting dressed, I was exhausted and ready to go back to bed. Instead, another therapist arrived at 7:30 to feed me my pureed breakfast and monitor my swallowing function. All my food had to be mashed up or blended because my throat muscles were so weak I could barely swallow. I couldn't even have a glass of water for fear of aspirating. All my beverages had a powder called

ThickenUp added that turned liquids into a gelatin substance within seconds. When I used to work out, I'd downed many energy shakes that weren't too tasty, but this was just gross. Growing up, my father used to tease us by asking if we wanted a cup of mud. This was pretty darn close!

Once a week, "swallow studies" and X rays were made of my throat to monitor changes. I was only able to eat such soft foods as oatmeal, applesauce, and mashed potatoes. Soon, I progressed to eating more solids like bananas, pears, and peaches. I quickly advanced from eating in my room to eating with my fellow patients in the gathering room.

My first morning there I was horrified. The room was filled with brain-injury patients. Most were stroke survivors, although some had suffered severe car accidents or sports injuries. One young man had been kicked in the head while playing soccer and wore a halo with screws in his head. Ouch! It gave me the willies to even look at him. We sat expressionless, strapped securely in our wheelchairs, slumped to one side. I lost my appetite watching everyone drooling saliva and food. To my horror, I was in the same condition.

We waited, with our food tray covered on the table in front of us, while a therapist made her way around the table, working with one patient at a time. She sat next to us, uncovered our food, and took notes about our ability to chew and swallow. Usually, a few bites was all I could manage.

After breakfast we had a short break and then I was
wheeled to the gym for physical therapy. Entering the
large open room for the first time, I just stared. Unlike
any gym I had ever seen, it was filled with large colored
balls, matted tables, and walkers. I was wheeled over to
one of the matted tables and introduced to my physical
therapist.

"Hi, Valerie," said a young woman with long blonde
hair. "My name is Christine, and I'm going to be your
physical therapist for the next few weeks."

She assisted me out of my wheelchair and onto the
table. I laid on my back while she assessed the condition
of my leg and arm. While she took notes, I looked around
and saw a patient learning to walk with only one leg and
others struggling to do the simplest things. Hanging my
head in despair, I wondered how I was ever going to
overcome this.

My 30-minute session with Christine was emotionally
exhausting. I wanted to leave. No, I wanted to crawl into
a hole and die. Instead, I was wheeled around the corner
to Speech Therapy.

The tiny speech therapy room wasn't much bigger
than a broom closet. As the nurse wheeled me through
the narrow doorway, she warned me to keep my hands
and elbows safely tucked in. A desk sat at the back of
the little room; the therapist swiveled her chair around
to face me as I entered. She was younger than me with
light auburn hair.

"Hi, I'm Beth, your speech therapist," she said, smiling and extending her hand for me to shake. Friendly and eager to help me, Beth was ready to get going. Not me. I was overwhelmed. I could hardly concentrate. All I could focus on was what I had lost: I couldn't move half of my body. I couldn't speak. I couldn't even make sounds.

It was like being buried alive. I was in there, but no one could hear me.

Several nights, I had horrible nightmares of being buried alive, trying to scream as I was being lowered into the ground. Terror at the sound of the dirt hitting the casket jolted me awake—chest pounding, covered in sweat.

I refused to leave my room for the next few days and would hardly eat. The nurses realized I was depressed and called the rehab doctor who prescribed a session with a psychologist. For some reason three showed up. I must have been a case study or something, to qualify for a private session with three shrinks. When they entered my room, one of them began to speak in a sympathetic, yet condescending manner.

"Ms. Greene—Valerie—we understand how difficult and frustrating this must be for you. We are here to offer our assistance as you work through accepting your limitations."

"Limitations!" I thought. "Ha! I'm not accepting any limitations! And how on earth can YOU even begin to understand my frustration?" Anger rose up inside me, sparking a flame. I motioned for my writing board, which they quickly handed me, eager to hear how I felt.

Earlier that year, a shocking story was aired on the
national news about a woman named Lorena Bobbit who,
after discovering her husband was cheating on her, cut off
his penis, took it for a drive, and threw it out the window.
Amazingly enough, his penis was found and surgically sewn
back on. He was later exalted on talk shows for starring in a
pornographic film. Apparently, his ego needed to
demonstrate how well his reattached parts worked.

I wrote fast and furiously, in all capital letters, and then
turned my board to face the three doctors. It said; "IF THEY
CAN FIX BOBBIT'S DICK, THEY CAN FIX ME!"

They just stood there. I'd never seen a group of
doctors so stunned. After a long silence, they left, one by
one, the last one snickering. They could see that I was
much more aware than they had realized and that I wasn't
going to accept any limitations.

More importantly, so did I. My anger had awakened my
fighting spirit–igniting the fire within. My depression
vanished, burned away by my anger. I would *not* just accept
these limitations! I was going to show them—I had this, "it"
didn't have me! As my heart pounded, I promised myself that
I would do everything in my power to overcome my
limitations and recover. I realized that I couldn't depend on
the doctors alone to change my situation–this would require
my involvement. I would do my best in rehab, work my
hardest. And I would search for health care professionals who
believed I could recover fully, ones who would do more than
just help me "accept my limitations."

Word of the incident traveled fast and one of the older, more mature nurses came to my room. "Honey, you are going to be fine," she said. "You are a fighter. The ones who fight get better. The quiet, complacent ones are the ones we worry about."

I returned to speech and physical therapy with a vengeance. My therapists and the nurses were excited over my returned motivation. I told myself I was going to overcome this, even if I died trying. All my life I had been told that the faith of a mustard seed can move a mountain; now was the time to find out.

CHAPTER FIVE

Finding My Voice

Before I could leave the hospital to go home, I would have to learn to speak.

Every Monday through Friday, at 9 a.m., I was moved from my bed to my wheelchair and taken to physical therapy. In the beginning, I had to rely solely on Christine to move my flaccid limbs until I was strong enough to crawl. Learning to crawl was—and still is—very difficult! But you must crawl before you can walk. I'd heard this, but never having children, I didn't know exactly why. Now I knew. The act of crawling creates a connection between the right and left hemispheres of the brain and

sets up the cross pattern that allows us to walk, read, and
do hundreds of other important tasks. In order to crawl, I
had to strengthen my muscles. One strengthening exercise
I remember well was reaching for small colored cones
while on my hands and knees. Christine would set the
cones just outside my reach and hold me up with a wide
belt secured around my waist as I leaned forward to pick
them up. This forced me to put weight on my weak leg,
knee, and arm. What once seemed like child's play
brought tears to my eyes as my body trembled.
Leaving the gym each day, I stared at the treadmill,
remembering my former workouts with my friends and
personal trainer and wondering if I'd ever be able to do
those things again.

The genuine concern of all my therapists was
extraordinary. They each seemed personally motivated to
see me walk again. As I held on to a set of parallel bars,
Christine would stand me up and move my paralyzed foot
one step at a time as another therapist held onto me. I was
determined to walk. They were careful not to cause any
unnecessary pain or discomfort, but it was evident that
my desire to overcome my injury mattered more to me
than any pain.

Each day following physical therapy, I went to speech
therapy. I especially looked forward to speech, because I
wanted to talk so badly. I prayed that my voice would
return so I could speak again, even promising God that I
would never stop talking if He would just give me my

voice back. Those who know me will attest that I'm a woman of my word!

In my first sessions, Beth taught me facial and oral exercises to strengthen my cheek and tongue muscles. Later, alone in my room, I practiced them over and over. One required pulling my tongue out with my hand while retracting it at the same time. The resistance creates strength. In my room, I did not have any gauze pads to hold my tongue, so I used my shirt. Naturally, this created a big wet spot on my shirt. Not pretty, but it worked. I think my tongue could pull a car.

Beth and I spent many hours with flash cards and puzzles, relearning how to identify numbers and pronounce the alphabet. As I slowly relearned my ABCs, the million dollar cases I used to work on for my clients seemed a lifetime ago. Even though it was frustrating to have to relearn everything, I was grateful that my memory and cognitive functions were returning.

One morning, Beth said, "Valerie, it's time to give up your writing board, so you can find your voice."

"No way," I thought. I'd only had my precious white board for a week. I had written on every piece of paper in sight until someone realized I needed one. It was my sole means of communicating! And now she wanted to take it away.

"No!" I wrote.

"It will be tough at first," Beth said as she reached for my board. "But this is how you will find your voice. And you'll only have to give it up when you are with me. I'll let you have it back after our session."

I lowered my head in humble acceptance as I handed her the board. She was right; it was tough! Several times I reached to write my answers and couldn't. As I began to make sounds, Beth commended me for my intense motivation.

"Valerie, this is hard work. It may not feel like you are making much progress yet, but you are. Your motivation is admirable. So many stroke survivors give up. We have a saying around here: 'Some become better and some become bitter.'"

That stuck with me. Despite my frustration, I did not want to become bitter. I practiced all the exercises she gave me and even tried reading out loud, while alone in my room. I picked up a magazine that someone had given to me and began to read the cover. I knew the words. I understood their meaning. I heard them in my head. But when they came out, the sounds were strange and made no sense.

"What on earth was that?" I thought. "When did I learn Russian?" Hearing myself try to read was frightening, but I had to laugh. The more I was able to laugh at myself, the stronger I felt. My fighting spirit was emerging. My stroke became my opponent. When struggling to speak or move, I would think "I'm not going to let you beat me, dammit! You picked the wrong girl."

I kept practicing my speech, and within a few weeks, I was beginning to sound out a few words. My first word was the one I had to be able to say before I could be discharged: "Help!"

One of my next words was rabbit—a fond memory. Growing up, I'd raised dwarf rabbits in my backyard. I started out with only one, then decided he needed a mate and—well—soon there were so many that I turned my backyard into a profit center, delivering baskets of adorable baby bunnies to the local pet stores at Easter. My parents were supportive of my entrepreneurial spirit, and grew equally fond of the furry little creatures. Now I practiced the word over and over, and when Angie arrived for her daily visit, I looked up at her and proudly shouted "RABBIT!"

"Val, you can talk!" she exclaimed.

"Rabbit," I agreed. "Rabbit!"

I progressed quickly, learning a new word every day. I finally learned how to say my name. That afternoon, in my room, I phoned a friend who didn't know I'd had a stroke. I was hoping that she would recognize me.

"Hello," she answered.

"V-v-v-v-aaaallllllll," I articulated, as clearly as I could, knowing I sounded like a 3-year-old child.

"Val, is that you?" she said. Tears filled my eyes. She knew it was me!

"Where are you?" she asked.

"H-h-h-oossspitttalll," I sounded out. The call didn't last long. I couldn't say much of anything, but a

connection was made. After we hung up, she called my
mother to find out what had happened.

All my life, I'd been competitive and strong. Now I was
speaking at the level of a 3-year-old. What had I been
reduced to? Little did I know that I was beginning a
whole new life—a rebirthing process.

Life had taken a dramatic change. Some days I'd sit in my
wheelchair outside the gym and watch as new patients arrived
with their families and went through orientation. I'd listen to
the nurse explain to the family what therapies to expect.

"In rehab we provide three different therapies: physical
therapy, better known as PT, occupational therapy or OT,
and speech," the nurse would say.

Listening to her recite the standard speech, I sighed.
Sometimes I felt like an old-timer. Having been there a
while, I had the lingo down pat. PT, which we patients
often referred to as physical torture, was obviously
working with your physical challenges. Speech was self-
explanatory, but occupational therapy, unlike the word
implies, has nothing to do with your occupation. OT
teaches you how to use your fine motor skills. This was
my least favorite and most frustrating therapy. It consisted
of repetitive tasks like picking up pennies, putting pegs in
a board, and identifying shapes with my eyes closed.
What a pain! But it was there that I learned to tie my
shoes, cook, and make my bed with one hand.

Afternoons were our free time. The first week, I stayed
in my room, isolated with my thoughts, until I drove

myself crazy. Soon I joined the other patients in the gathering room to make crafts. Painting pottery and making hot plates were nowhere near my former interests, but you'd never have known it. I was having a good time. It was my sister who was freaking out as she watched me making crafts.

"This is too strange; this is not my sister," Angie told the nurse. "Valerie doesn't do crafts. She hates crafts. Valerie would no more be caught making crafts than I would be fishing. Is this permanent? Is she going to snap out of this?"

My poor sister. Her nerves were shot. She didn't know whether to laugh or cry. It was true. I was different. Like a child, I was having fun.

Once a week, we had a group therapy session. It was there that we shared our stories about our strokes. When it was my turn to share my story, the therapist explained that my voice was temporarily down for repairs. Instead, I was exalted as an excellent listener.

I felt safe with the other patients and grew to care about them. Even though most of them were 30 to 40 years older than me, we'd all endured a life altering experience that bonded us together. One lady had her stroke while riding her John Deere tractor, mowing her property. Almost every time I saw her, she asked me, "When you get out of here, will you go mow my yard?" Another elderly woman had laid on her floor for three days, just 2 feet from her phone, until her housekeeper found her.

**Val in gathering room participating in
group therapy**

I was concerned about the prognosis of some of my older friends. I knew leaving them would be hard.

A bulletin board posted all the extra activities available. Haircuts were scheduled on Tuesdays between 1 and 4 p.m. Because my hair was frightful, I signed up for a hospital haircut. Not something endorsed by Vidal Sassoon or any hair professional. The volunteer was very nice but much older than any hairdresser I had known. Being the yuppie that I was, this was horrifying to me but like everything else, I was learning to surrender and go with the flow. In only seconds, my hair went from shoulder length to above my ears without any shape or style. I looked dreadful. I might as well have been bald. I left the room humiliated, still wearing my cap. How I would have loved a new "do" from Douglas Marvaldi—my long-time hairdresser who I referred to as the godfather of hair.

Although my prognosis was uncertain, I was determined to make my own outcome, regardless of what any doctor or pamphlet might say. In fact, I threw away the "Stroke Care" manual that was given to me. I didn't want to fill my head with thoughts and pictures of what to expect. I wanted to create my own experience. Of course, my caretakers had to be aware of the effects of stroke so they could be prepared to care for me properly. But, I strongly believe that we manifest the things we dwell on. I wanted to focus on how I could make myself better as quickly as possible.

Nearing the end of my extended stay, I was given a catalog to pick out my wheelchair. The chairs came in all kinds of designs and colors. As I turned the pages, my anger grew. I did not intend to live my life in a wheelchair! I would not accept that as an option! I closed the catalog and slung it out into the hallway as far as it could go. Thunk! It smacked against the wall across from my open door.

The nurses were very understanding about my anger. And, thank God, they were tolerant of my mischievousness. Single-handedly, I kept the staff on their toes! I was always trying to escape from the rehab wing. My room was located at the far end of a hallway that was closed off by double automated doors. Each day after lunch, I would sit in my

wheelchair in the doorway of my room and watch the
doctors and nurses enter and exit through the double doors
that led out to the main lobby and cafeteria. Watching their
daily routine, I memorized their shifts and learned that
during the lunch hours they would leave the doors open for
about 10 minutes. The sounds of shuffling feet and the
aroma of fresh-baked chocolate chip cookies filled the
hallways just outside those doors.

I longed to be able to go get one of those cookies;
finally the day came to make my move. I worked my
wheelchair with my good leg and edged out of my room
into the hallway, and waited. Sure enough, just like
clockwork, the shift returning from lunch left the doors
open for ten minutes. Off I went.

Once I made it through the doors, I slowly wheeled
myself down the hall. I was doing fine until I came to an
area where the floor sloped down.

What a bizarre design in a hospital! Easing my way
slowly, I kept my good foot against the floor to control
the speed of my wheelchair, and managed to make it
safely down the slope. At the bottom was the cafeteria.

Entering, I thought, "What a woman will do for
chocolate!"

The self-service counter was low enough for my
wheelchair so I managed to get a few cookies and a small
pint of milk. Going through the checkout line, I
presented my patient ID. Since patients did not need to
pay, the clerk waved me through and I proceeded to a

nearby table to enjoy my cookies and milk. Just being surrounded by real food was heavenly. My senses were going crazy. I could smell pizza, coffee, and lots of fresh-baked chocolate chip cookies!

After nearly an hour had passed, the nurses discovered that I was missing from my room, and the search began. Much to my dismay, it wasn't long before I heard my name being called, and I was found.

After being lectured, I realized that my escape was not the best decision I could have made. There were many things that could have happened to me, like falling down or injuring myself. But those things never entered my mind.

When I returned to PT the next morning, my little escapade had made the "headlines" among the therapists. Somehow, I remained in good standing with the staff, even though they did seem to check my room more often.

As the weeks of rigorous therapy continued, I grew stronger both mentally and physically. One day, Angie hung a large bow on my door and said I was being crowned a "star patient." Ha! A "star pain" was probably more like it! This was my sister's psychology at work: She was just hoping I would live up to being a star patient.

During my last week, I received a visit from my childhood boyfriend, Milton. We'd met in first grade. He was a cute boy with curly hair. At our class Christmas party, our mothers met and became friends. His mother Edith was refined and classy. She wore mink coats and drove a Cadillac; they lived in a big house with a pool, which was a rare luxury back then. As our mothers grew to be best friends, Milton and I seemed to always be together.

I was surprised when I saw his home for the first time: He had told me he lived on a huge farm that was so big he hunted bears on his property. It must have seemed that way to him, but it was only an acre lot with lots of oak trees. The next Christmas, when our second grade teacher expressed a desire for a classroom tree, Milton raised his hand and offered to cut a tree from his property for the class. Then he whispered to me that he would give me a Christmas tree as well. His mother later shared that they'd had to buy three trees that year—one for them, one for the class, and one for me.

In school, Milton was mischievous, earning frequent paddlings from the teacher. One day, after a hard paddling, he walked by my desk and winked, lifting a wad of playing cards out of his pockets to show me what he had used to keep it from hurting.

We were both imaginative and loved to play outdoors. I loved riding in his three wheeler pretending to be Bonnie and Clyde racing up and down the unpaved street surrounding his rural home. But, like any two kids, we would get on each other's nerves at times and would have to be separated. Our mothers always hoped that one day we would marry. Now he stood next to my wheelchair, holding out flowers.

Looking at his warm smile, unable to speak, I could only cry.

"Valerie, when you get out of here, I'll take you to my doctor. I know he can help you. You can beat this!"

I believed him and hung on to his message of hope.

On Fridays, there was a weekly meeting with all my doctors and therapists to discuss my progress. Family members were allowed to attend, but none of mine were able. Our family friend Eloise attended in their absence. Angie had to return to Pensacola to care for her young son. Michelle was pregnant and working full-time as a legal assistant in Maryland. Eloise was a reflexologist. She came several times a week to give me foot massages. She taught me that rubbing the bottom of your big toes

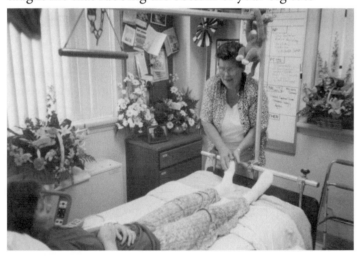

Eloise giving Valerie a reflexology treatment

stimulates the brain and blood flow. The weekly meetings were semiformal. Eloise and I sat silently at the conference table while the doctors and therapists took turns discussing my progress. It felt like they were grading me—

and they were. At the end of the meeting, I was asked if I had anything I would like to add. Each time I would nod my head and write the word "Home" on a sheet of paper.

I was so homesick! Fortunately Angie and Michelle had decorated my hospital room to make it feel more homey. A wind chime that Michelle bought me hung from the overhead rail of my bed, and a sound machine filled the room with the pleasant sounds of crickets at night and a peaceful ocean throughout the day. Passing doctors would stop to comment on how they were coming back to my room to relax! A framed photograph of my cat Alex sat on my dresser. Flowers and get-well cards covered every shelf and available floor space. At one point I started giving them to other patients.

My heart went out to a teenage girl who'd been severely injured and lost an eye in a terrible car accident. She was lucky to be alive, but I knew sometimes she didn't feel that way. Every day, during my free time, I'd wheel myself down to her room and look in the door to see if she was awake and up for company. She would wave and gesture that I could come in. Neither of us could talk, but we were able to communicate. We were the youngest patients in the unit and had an unspoken bond.

The Fourth of July came and I watched the downtown fireworks from a hospital window. Tears streamed down my face as I reminisced about the good times I had, surrounded by friends in past years.

Returning to my room, I tried phoning friends, but because I could only make a few garbled sounds, they had no way of knowing it was me and would hang up. Hearing their voices made me feel like I was still in the same world, only on another side. This saddened me greatly.

Each night I would thank God for helping me make it through another day, and ask for the strength and courage to make it through the next. I was especially grateful for my sister Angie. I knew that no matter what happened, she would care for me. I'll never forget how I would wait each day by my hospital window to see her silver minivan pull up to the curb to take me out for a couple of hours. As promised, she came as often as she was able, faithful and reliable. Taking my wheelchair apart she would help the nurses lift me into the front seat of her van.

Sometimes we would just ride down Park Avenue, a lovely street of shops, cafés, and restaurants, or simply ride by my house. It did not matter where we went; I was just happy to get out.

A little over a month had passed and I was told that my discharge had been authorized for the coming week with a home health care nurse and outpatient rehabilitation program. I was elated! I was finally going *home!*

After what seemed like the slowest weekend in my life, Monday morning arrived. Sitting on my bed, packed and fully dressed, I waited for my sister to come and take me home. Upon her arrival, she collected my discharge orders and papers. If you have ever stayed in a hospital, you know that this can take forever. While I was waiting, I sprayed my room with an entire can of pink Silly String! Michelle had given it to me in a care package she'd sent. I'm sure she didn't expect me to use it indoors, but it was fun and helped express my joy.

When Angie came to get me, I insisted that we stop in every room to say good-bye to the friends I had made during my long stay. I cried as I hugged each person, knowing that I might not ever see them again. I had bonded with my fellow stroke survivors, the outstanding, dedicated nurses who had cared for me, and the amazing therapists who pushed me in spite of my tears and frustration. Before leaving, we made one last stop at the gift shop, where I purchased something for each of the nurses and staff who had cared for me. I had no words to express my gratitude; I hoped my gifts would help them understand. They'd helped me begin the process of reclaiming my life. Now I would have to find a way to continue on my own.

CHAPTER SIX

Home!

> On July 12, 1996, I finally returned to my lovely home, a day I'd longed for. It would prove more difficult than I'd imagined, but it was my first step toward recovering my independence.

Coming home, I felt like a wounded soldier returning home from war. Angie wheeled me down the long brick walkway that led to my two-story house. My friend Tom had built a ramp so she could get my wheelchair up the stairs of my front porch. Entering the front door, I smelled the familiar scents of home—mahogany furniture, candles, and wood floors.

Just beyond the tall columns that framed the formal dining room, Alex peered at me from the den. Out of instinct, I tried to call him. But I couldn't say his name. Rather than jumping in my lap as usual, he turned and ran. Disappointed, I was sure that it was just a matter of time before my faithful furry friend would come around.

I learned to survive, one day at a time. Angie was able to stay with me for only a few days, as she had to return to her family. Before she left, she arranged for a nurse from a local service to come each morning to bathe and dress me and return each evening to help me get ready for bed.

Sherri, the nurse, was very supportive. She was in her early forties and had a strong build. Like a good caretaker, she was very nurturing and always looking out for my safety. I wasn't always easy to care for; I had refused most of the hospital's home health care products like the white plastic shower chair. It would have been easier to use, but it was just "wrong" sitting in my elegant black tub. So Sherri assisted me into and out of the bath.

It was good to have her there with me every morning and evening. I needed the emotional support as much as I needed the physical help. Even though I no longer had to use my walker, and could transfer in and out of my wheelchair, I was unable to stand on my own.

My beautiful remodeled 1800s Key West-style house had a steep stairway with a single banister on one side; the other side was left open to the dining room as a design feature. My physical therapist had strongly advised me to avoid the stairs, but my beautiful bedroom and office beckoned me to come up. Besides, I loved the feeling that being upstairs gave me. I felt like I was in a tree house; it brought back fond childhood memories of my tree forts. Growing up, I lived across the street from a heavily wooded piece of property where my friends and I enjoyed building and playing in our tree forts high above the ground.

I was determined to be able to use the stairs and enjoy my beautiful bedroom and office. So I would wheel my chair over to the stairs and slide myself onto the first step. With my strong right arm, I'd hold onto the banister and pull myself up one step at a time. My arm was still strong from all my former workouts. But the left side of my body was heavy and weak. Each week when my housekeeper Maxine came, she would scrub the marks off the wood floors and stairs that were made by my dragging foot. She was always sure to tell me how good I was doing and encourage me to keep up the hard work.

I often wished that family or friends could stay with me during the days and especially the long nights. It was frightening to wake up at night, choking on my saliva. The stroke had paralyzed my soft palate, and swallowing was difficult. It was especially scary when I woke up in the night unable to breathe, saliva down my windpipe. When that had happened in the hospital, the nurses had come running to help me. Now, at home, I would slide off the bed and crawl to the door. Pulling myself up by the doorknob I would lean against the wall for support as I made my way down the long hallway to the bathroom, gagging and choking. Sometimes it would take 30 minutes before I could stop choking and breathe normally.

Other times I'd wake at night, having to go to the bathroom. Again, I'd work my way down the long hallway by myself. Sometimes I wouldn't make it in time, and I'd wet myself. I'd be up for the next hour, changing into dry clothes and crawling back to bed. At times like this, I felt so alone, so abandoned. I needed help so badly. Often I would cry myself back to sleep. Other times I was angry. Why did this have to happen to me? Why do I have to do this all by myself? Taking care of myself took all my strength and courage.

Before the stroke, my days were frantically full. Now they were slow and boring. My big outings were my two-hour sessions at the Outpatient Rehab Center on Mondays, Wednesdays, and Fridays. On those mornings, a small red-and-white bus picked me up at my house, and then picked up several other shut-ins who did not have assistance, and took us all to our therapy sessions. The bus was a public service provided by the city if you qualified. Other than those sessions, most of my time was idle.

Thank God for my faithful friends who came by to bring me food and visit. I was so grateful for their support and genuine kindness. But I was terribly hurt by the many I'd considered friends who never came by or even tried to call. It wasn't until years later, while working through my emotional trauma, that I forgave them, realizing they must have been overwhelmed by fear.

I spent hours sitting alone in my wheelchair in front of the TV or staring out the window. The loneliness became unbearable. At times, I felt it had a presence, like a demon, lurking all around me, engulfing me. It made me feel useless and unwanted. Many nights I laid awake wondering why God had allowed me to live to be so injured and so lonely. Why didn't He just let me die? Taking my own life entered my mind. I knew I would be missed greatly by my family and friends, but I felt they would understand. This just wasn't me. I felt like a burden to my loved ones—and that feeling was unbearable.

Whenever I was haunted by these thoughts, I always heard an inner voice telling me not to give up. I knew in my heart that I was alive for a reason, that my journey was not complete.

There were many signs that this stroke was an important part of my life path, almost as if I'd been prepared for it. With hindsight, they are easy to see. Prior to my stroke, when I'd work out, I felt as though I was training for something besides having a good figure. Doing leg lunges down a long hall with weights until I fell with exhaustion and arm curls till my biceps popped out, I had pushed myself to becoming extremely strong. Now as I pulled my body weight up the stairs with one arm, I was grateful for that strength.

I also realized that my first grade teacher had played a part in my destiny.

She had insisted that I learn to use my right hand instead of my left.

"No one else in the class writes with their left hand," she would say. Scared to appear different or to go against her wishes, I forced myself to switch my natural writing hand. If it hadn't been for this, I would be left handed— and unable to communicate after the stroke. How grateful I am for that gift! I'd watched many of my fellow stroke survivors try to learn to write with their nondominant hand, and it was hard.

It was also a good thing I'd never been a big eater. Food wasn't a necessity to me, and I didn't need much. Now my meals consisted of anything available and accessible. Before she'd left, Angie had stocked my kitchen with lots of easy-to-open foods like yogurt, fruit mix, and banana pudding—my favorite! I quickly discovered all the things that are impossible to do one handed: Peel a banana, open a can, or cut food. My natural survivor instincts kicked in, and I learned to use my teeth as a tool to assist me. But some things were impossible, like opening a bag of potato chips, reaching for something in the freezer, or on a shelf. For those things, I had to wait until Maxine or Sherri arrived, humbled and frustrated at not being able to do it myself.

My friend Tom was unemployed at the time, and he would drive me anywhere I wanted to go. I agreed to buy his meals in exchange for him driving me. It worked out for both of us. He was great company for me, and he got to eat out a lot. At the time, I was embarrassed to be seen in public, so I selected restaurants that my friends were less likely to frequent. I often chose the Holiday House, where my father had taken my family on Sundays after church when we were children. He would ask for a table near the large window that overlooked the racetrack so we could watch the horses practice while we ate. The restaurant had now lost its former grandeur, but they were still famous for their extraordinary pies and cakes. Their banana cake was my favorite. Since many of the customers were elderly, my disability did not stand out, and I could relax.

When Tom wasn't available to go to dinner, I'd fax a delivery request to Pizza Hut, ordering a small Supreme pan pizza. This yuppie was not going to starve!

As I relearned how to take care of myself, I noted how attentive Alex was to me. He was far more than a pet. He'd been with me for 7 years, since he was a kitten, and we had always been close. Alex walked on a leash and loved riding in the car, especially down Park Avenue, wearing his leopard scarf. He even flew with me when I traveled. Before my stroke, he seemed to be more independent and enjoyed his time alone napping on the deck in the shade. But now he never left my side. Every night he would run to the top of the stairs and wait for me as I pulled myself up each step, one by one. Once I reached the top of the staircase, he would run to my bedroom and wait for me on my bed and stay with me throughout the night until my nurse arrived in the morning.

Since I'd come home, his attentiveness increased to the point that I believed he was an angel in disguise. He seemed to watch over and protect me. At times, I felt that we communicated by reading each other's thoughts.

Our home was designed with French doors that ran along the entire back of the den, overlooking the back deck. I loved looking out at the palms and tropical red flowers that covered the wooden privacy fence in my backyard. The view reminded me of my trip to Tahiti only a few years prior. One evening while I was sitting in the den reading, I heard Alex growling as he stared out the French doors. For a cat, and especially Alex, that was very odd. I had only heard him hiss maybe a dozen times in his life. But growl? Never. He was obviously scared. And, now, so was I. What could be outside those doors? Alex's eyes grew wider.

When I looked out the door, I saw nothing at first.

"What do you see?" I asked Alex.

He continued to growl. Obviously, it was still there; I just couldn't see it. Then, in the lower left side of the door I saw it. A little furry bandit wearing a mask.

"Oh Alex, it's only a raccoon." I was relieved.

I reached for the door and tossed an Oreo cookie to the little fellow. I had never seen one up close. He was adorable! I watched as he held the cookie in his front paws and devoured it.

The next night, as I sat watching TV, Alex began to growl. Our little visitor was back. But, this time he had brought with him his entire family: brothers, sisters, aunts, uncles, and cousins. Big and small; they covered every inch of the deck. It was like Alfred Hitchcock's movie *The Birds*, except with raccoons.

Now what? We were out numbered—20 to 1. As I reached for the bag of cookies, Alex reared up and looked at me. I swear he was talking to me telepathically.

"Do NOT open that door!"

I hesitated.

OK, maybe I shouldn't, I thought. It was a bit spooky. They did look like gremlins with a plan, especially the big ones.

The neighborhood was safe and, like most of Winter Park, safety was taken very seriously. So when a letter arrived warning us about a rabid raccoon on the loose, I was bewildered. I was completely oblivious to what this meant. I tilted my head, puzzled at the word "rabid." Perhaps they had misspelled rabbit.

"A rabbit and a raccoon mated? Big deal," I thought, tossing the flyer in the garbage.

At times, I felt like a kid living alone, not sure what to do or expect. My "filters," my protective instincts, had been removed and I had become very innocent. My guard was down. And what was worse, I didn't realize it.

Weeks passed and I asked a friend to arrange for a limousine to pick me up and take me out for the evening. If I had learned one thing, it was that life is short and you'd better enjoy it while you can. So I was going to make the best of it.

Upon arriving at my house, I handed the limo driver a written explanation of my disability and a list of my destination requests. He drove me down Park Avenue and to

one of my favorite cafés to buy ice cream. I stayed in the limo
as he went inside to take my order. We drove around most of
the evening, riding past familiar places that brought back
fond memories. It was 9 p.m. when we returned to the
house. The driver, John, opened the car door and helped me
out. I used my cane, and he held my left arm, as we made
our way up the brick walkway to the house.

The ride had been relaxing and allowed me to forget
my troubles for a while.

Later that night after I had gone to bed, I was
awakened by the phone ringing at 2 a.m. I picked up the
phone and listened.

"Hi, Valerie," said a slightly familiar male voice. "This
is John, your limo driver. I'm coming over to visit you;
I'll be there in a few minutes."

Unable to respond, I quickly hung up the phone and
dialed 9-1-1. I was frightened. No one visits at that hour,
especially not your limo driver. As soon as someone answered
the 9-1-1 call, I could only say in a faint voice, *"Help."*

Police officers arrived shortly after my call and walked
throughout my house and yard. They did not see anyone.
They left their card and insisted that I call if he phoned
again. Fortunately, I never heard from him again, nor did
I pursue any limo reservations for a while.

Day after day, I'd sit on my front porch swing, waiting
for the mailman or for a visitor and hoping to see a
familiar face. Alex sat, curled next to me. One morning,
to my surprise, a truck pulled up in the mulch drive. It

was Milton! He had come to fulfill his promise. I was so happy to see him. He told me he was taking me to see that special doctor he knew. He put my wheelchair into his truck, and we drove off. Arriving at a large office building, he carefully pushed me in my wheelchair up the ramp and into the elevator.

While sitting in the waiting room, I looked over various magazines and brochures outlining the alternative procedures in which the doctor specialized. Some of them I recognized. But I had no idea what *live stem cell injections* or *hyperbaric oxygen treatments* were. Growing up, my mother was very health conscious. We had our traditional family physician, but she always sought holistic treatments to complement our care. Having this influence as a child, I learned to be open but cautious. Not all care, whether traditional or holistic, is good care. But now, my choices were limited. I refused to stay in the condition I was in. I desperately needed help, and I was trusting God that I had found it. Moments later, the nurse came out and said that we could see the doctor. Winding down a long hallway, past many rooms, we came to a large office at the end of the hall. The walls were covered with traditional framed degrees, but his office was eccentrically decorated with a red sofa and animal skins. Sitting behind a large glass desk was a man wearing a white lab coat and cowboy boots. Hmmm…different.

He peered around a microscope, welcomed us, and asked how he could help. Since I was still unable to speak well,

Milton explained my condition. The doctor looked at me with compassion and described the program he offered and how it could help me. It required leaving the country for a month and going to an offshore medical facility that he owned and operated in the Dominican Republic. The program had been noted for its overwhelming results with stroke patients and severe injuries.

In addition to a stack of magazine articles that he was highlighted in, he gave us the name of a former patient—a trial lawyer in a city not far from where I lived. I jotted a note requesting that I would like to hear about this patient's experience. So the doctor phoned the patient. The man's wife answered the phone. The doctor explained the reason for his call and told her about my injury. She shared the story of how her injured husband was at the point of suicide—until he returned, dramatically improved, after having the treatment. After hearing her testimony, coupled with the many endorsements I had read, I was convinced of his credibility and filled with hope.

Unfortunately, the program was not covered by insurance and the cost was more than I had available or that anyone in my family could manage at the time. And because the best results are achieved as soon after an injury as possible, time was of the essence. What would I do? Discouraged, I didn't know how I could go without the necessary funds.

A few days passed and my friends Lori and Helen, my business and golfing buddies, heard of my need. Helen owned an AllState insurance agency in Winter Park; Lori was a broker with a large insurance firm. They went into action, arranging a golf tournament and auction to raise money. They gathered impressive donations from celebrities and local businesses, many of whom had once been clients of my firm and were eager to help.

Over a hundred people came to be part of the event. Even a local sports celebrity was there and signed autographs. Angie had come for the occasion and was given a large hat that had been donated by a local designer. It was an amazing collaboration of rhinestones and bows. I'm surprised it didn't play music! With her long blonde hair, she wore it well.

Words will never be able to express the amount of love and support I felt that day and how my spirits were lifted. Nearly all of the money that I needed for the treatment was raised.

A trust was formed and plane reservations were made. I had one week to get any last minute things in order. I was leaving the country to undergo *live stem cell treatments*. Unsure of what to expect, I put all my fear aside and trusted God to take care of me.

My long time friend and veterinarian Dr. Sandy Fink, offered to care for Alex while I was away. Pat Peters, my massage therapist agreed to accompany me through my first week of treatment because neither of my sisters could make the trip due to other obligations. My mother was still not speaking to me, and my father had just started on a new business venture and was unable to leave. Pat was someone I enjoyed being around. She was a kind, older woman whom I trusted. Having her companionship was a great comfort to me.

Preparing for the trip, I was both anxious and scared. I was uncertain how my body would respond to the treatment or how I would manage in a foreign place. All I knew for sure was that I felt watched over and protected.

Dr. Fink came by my house to pick up Alex. With tears streaming down my face, I held my dear pet tightly and kissed him good-bye. My throat burned from the pain of not knowing if it was the last time I would see him. My only comfort was knowing that he would be in good hands.

My nurse helped pack my suitcase with the barest of necessities. Workout attire was about the only clothing that I could wear because I couldn't yet manage zippers or buttons. A photograph of Alex was among the few mementos I took to remind me of home.

CHAPTER SEVEN

A Medical Miracle

> My fears about leaving home and spending
> a month in a foreign country were
> outweighed by my desire to recover.

Arriving in Miami's busy airport, Pat pushed me in my
wheelchair to the gate and up to the plane. It was a tiny
30-seat plane—a puddle jumper, as I call them. I was
assisted to my seat and buckled up. Closing my eyes, I
visualized a red carpet being rolled ahead of us, all the way
to our destination with angels standing on each side. I
stayed focused on this visual until our tiny plane touched
down on the island of the Dominican Republic, just off
the coast of Florida. As we landed, all of the Dominicans

on the plane started clapping—their traditional way of thanking the pilot.

Entering the island airport, I was reminded of a similar airport in the Bahamas that I had visited as a young girl, with my father. It was a small open-air building in which you could easily see from one side to the other. Pat waved for a bellboy to collect our luggage, and then we proceeded to the outside curb. I stared in amazement at the interesting taxicabs that were lined up on the dusty drive, waiting for customers. The choices were quite unique. There were old army jeeps with no tops and VW Beetles with fringe hanging from the headliners, miniature statues of Christ on the dashboards, and crucifixes hanging from the rearview mirrors. Most of the drivers were dressed in sandals and baggy linen pants. The heat was intense and the humidity was far more than I had ever experienced in Florida.

Looking around, we saw a dark-skinned native man standing in front of a van, holding a sign bearing my name. Pat waved to him, and he came over to us. Introducing himself in broken English, he pointed at the sign he was holding, with my name on it, to confirm it was me.

"*Buenos dias*, I'm Sammy. I drive you to clinic."

He proceeded to load our luggage into the van, and then wheel my chair onto the lift and get me situated in the back of the van. It was a customized van from the late seventies, with a bench sofa in the back and large panel windows on each side. All that was missing was shag carpet and Sonny and Cher.

As Sammy started the van, he turned on the radio. The lively Spanish music set the mood for the ride and off we went. He drove unusually fast down a rough two-lane asphalt road that had no lines. We were about 30 minutes away from the *Hospital of Americas* Plaza, located on the north coast of the Dominican Republic.

As we sped past miles of sugarcane fields, I saw children and adults walking along the roadside carrying long machetes over their shoulders. Sammy managed to explain to us, in gestures and broken English, that they were workers on their return home from the sugarcane fields. Approaching the small village where the medical facility was located, we drove through a tall set of iron gates that were guarded by soldiers dressed in full fatigues, holding machine guns. This was a bit alarming. I was confused. Where were we? I looked at Pat with concern, and she asked Sammy about the guards.

"Over there...Haiti," he pointed. "Not safe. No worries. Safe where you going. Tourist area heavily guarded."

On the other side of the gates, conditions drastically changed. Now instead of donkeys and thatched houses lining the road, the grounds were beautifully landscaped with towering palms and bright flowers. It was a stark change, almost like walking out of a ghetto and into a Disney theme park. This area was obviously a popular

tourist destination. Resorts surrounded a plush golf
course that centered the village where the *Hospital of
Americas* Plaza was located.

Sammy stopped the van at the plaza. Even though my
treatments would not begin until the next day, I'd been
told to go to the clinic before I checked into my room at
the hotel. The Polynesian-style plaza was filled with shops
and restaurants on the first floor, with the clinic on the
second floor along with other business offices. Pat
wheeled me to the elevator and we proceeded up.

When the elevator doors opened, we faced the clinic
entrance. Through the double glass doors, we could see
the receptionist awaiting our arrival. Cadie was a native of
the Dominican Republic, a young pretty girl with long
dark hair and a beautiful smile. She had learned English
from her American fiancé and could write and speak
fluently. She would be our translator. As she gave us a tour
of the facility, she explained that each room was dedicated
to a specific type of treatment depending on each patient's
protocol. Most all the rooms had large floor-to-ceiling
windows with spectacular views of the mountains and
ocean. I later learned this was designed purposefully to
give the patients a peaceful and positive outlook to focus
on. It became obvious that our environment played a vital
role in our recovery—something I wish the hospital back
home had known.

After the orientation, Sammy drove us to our hotel,
located down the street. The resort hotel was a series of

villas, one dedicated specifically for patients of the clinic.
Pat checked us in. Fortunately the desk clerk spoke
English and easily exchanged our money into their
currency. A bellboy drove us in a golf cart down the brick
path to our room. As he brought in our luggage, I looked
around the simple room. It was neat and clean,
containing only two double beds, a dresser, and a TV.
We'd been advised not to drink the tap water so Pat went
to the hotel gift shop and bought some bottled water.

Returning to the room, she helped me out of my
wheelchair and into bed to relax from the trip. I was
exhausted after the long day of travel. I longed for a hot
shower but this was impossible since I was unable to stand
on my own. I laid down on the bed to rest for a moment
and fell fast asleep.

Around 3 in the morning, I woke up vomiting
profusely. I was lying flat on my back and unable to turn.
Within seconds I began gagging and gasping for air.
Hearing me, Pat awoke and jumped out of her bed and
quickly came to my rescue. She turned my head and
cleared my air passageway. My neck was weak and limp.
Even my eyelids were too weak to open. I was having a
seizure. She held me through my convulsions and waited,
rubbing my back, telling me I would be OK. Once again,
I knew I was at death's door, and so did Pat. This time
there was no one we could call. We had not yet met the
doctors or nurses who would be providing my care, and
the clinic and the front desk were closed. So all we could

do was to wait. It wasn't long before my convulsions ceased and Pat was able to change my shirt and wash off my face. Exhausted, I passed out and slept till morning.

Morning arrived as a bright beam of sunlight burst through the tiny opening between the draperies. It was like a message from God, letting me know that I had survived the night and that a new day awaited me. Pat was up and ready to get me going. We were both eager to begin my treatment. Sammy arrived and loaded me into the van, with the automatic wheelchair lift. Sitting in the chair, I hung my head in humiliation as the tourists stared in curiosity.

Arriving at the medical plaza, we proceeded into the elevator and to the second floor. Cadie greeted us and took me to the changing room, where I was dressed in a green surgical top, and matching drawstring bottoms. She removed my diamond stud earrings and gave them to Pat for safekeeping. Wheeled into the next room, I was assisted out of my wheelchair and into a comfortable recliner and served my first meal.

Breakfast consisted of two hard-boiled eggs, unbuttered wheat toast, and papaya juice. The server was very polite, and like most of the staff, did not speak a word of English. Thankfully, his expressions were lovingly clear as he smiled and gestured that I should eat up. After breakfast, my vitals were taken and I was started on a *chelation IV* prepared specifically for my body chemistry. Island music played softly in the background as I sat in a recliner for an hour watching the clear IV bag disperse the concoction slowly into my veins.

Throughout the day I went from room to room receiving several comprehensive therapeutic treatments that included: *acupressure, chelation, color laser therapy, colonics, live stem cell injections, ionized oxygen breathing,* and *hyperbaric oxygen (HBO) therapy.*

I'll never forget the first time I saw the *hyperbaric oxygen* chamber. In the middle of an all white room sat a large tank with dials and buttons running down the side.

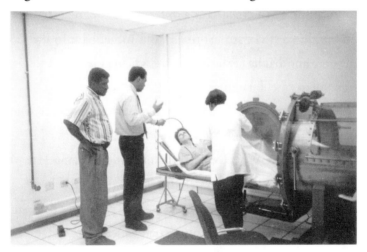

Val being placed inside chamber

It looked like a large steel coffin. A technician in a white jacket was seated on a stool facing the dials and meters. The back of the tank was open and a long flat metal tray extended out from it. As I stared in bewilderment, too stunned to ask any questions, the staff physician came in.

"Good morning, Valerie. I'm Dr. Alcedevez. Just call me
Dr. 'A' for short. It will be easier for you to say. The
procedure you are about to undergo is very simple. You just
lie in this tank and breathe normally. You won't feel or smell
anything. There is a window for you to look out, and
someone will always be sitting right here watching you. You'll
be in there for two hours every day, so you may want to
watch a video. We have a video player, but unfortunately, we
only have a couple of videos and they are both in Spanish."

I was then given a liquid tranquilizer to relax me, I laid on
the metal tray, and then I slid into the tank with the opening
shut behind me. I could hear a drill securing the bolts tight
on the closed steel door. Normally, this would have freaked
me out, but thanks to the *valerian*, I was in la-la land, too
tranquil to care. Like the *live stem cell injections,* the
hyperbaric oxygen tank was vital to my recovery; it delivered
oxygen to areas of poor circulation and tissue damage.

Waving to the group of doctors and nurses from inside the
tank, I began to relax and watch *The Terminator* video. It was
funny watching it in Spanish, and I quickly picked up the
language. When my two hours of confinement in the chamber
were over, I heard the drill opening the bolts on the door.

"*Hasta la vista,* baby!" I said to Dr. A, as I emerged.
Everyone just laughed. Oddly, I found speaking Spanish
easier than speaking English.

It wasn't long before I grew close to the staff, especially
Dr. A, who monitored all my treatments. He was
compassionate and understood my need for reassurance.

Only a few days had passed since our arrival, when an emergency alert was sounded, announcing that Hurricane Hortense, a Category 4 hurricane, was rapidly approaching the island. The 140 m.p.h. winds and ravaging rains had lashed Puerto Rico, less than 50 miles away, causing widespread destruction. Now the storm took dead aim at the tiny island of the Dominican Republic. Tourists scrambled to catch departing flights and evacuate the island before nightfall.

Having worked so hard to get there and being in the early stage of my treatment, I did not want to leave. Fortunately, Pat agreed with my decision and was willing to stick it out with me. After all, we were from Florida and used to tropical storms, or so we thought.

I probably would have stayed even if Pat didn't. There was no way I was boarding a tiny plane only to get tossed around in the sky and be nauseous for days. I had very intense memories of getting sick, and I'd rather die than go through that again.

We knew the force of a hurricane would do damage to the area and that the power might go out. So, Pat bought candles, water, bananas, and peanut butter. By evening the storm set in. Furious 130 m.p.h. winds tore through the island, tearing through the bamboo and palms surrounding our villas. We did not have a radio, and the TV was just static. Pat kept our draperies closed in case the winds broke the glass. The lights flickered as the power lines were damaged by the heavy winds.

Still, we felt safe, as though we were protected by angels. We knew we had not come this far to be run off by any hurricane. Throughout the night we listened to the howling wind tear through the hall outside our door. The eye of the hurricane was within 25 miles when, miraculously, it turned to the northeast, just missing us.

The next morning debris lay everywhere. Cars were stranded in the high pools of water, trees were down, and everyone was assessing the brutal beating that the high winds and 20 inches of rain had inflicted. There were reports of mudslides, in the upper regions of the island and in nearby villages that had adversely affected many people. I watched the natives working to clean up the debris, wondering if my driver would be able to get through to pick us up and take us to the clinic. But, just like clockwork, he was there at 8 a.m. sharp, waving and asking in his broken English if we were OK.

Resuming my treatment at the clinic, I continued to show signs of improvement. While all the treatments were beneficial, the primary reason I went to an offshore clinic was to receive *live stem cell injections,* also known as *embryonic cell stimulation.* This scientific breakthrough uses live cells from an embryo to replace injured or dead cells. In spite of promising results in other countries, the United States had not, at that time, begun to offer stem cell therapy as an approved, or legal, method of treatment. Few people realize that stem cells are available from sources other than human embryos. Mine were from a lamb.

It has been discovered that animal species in the embryo stage are identical to human cells until the time of species differentiation. In other words, a lamb embryo will look like a human embryo until it becomes old enough to differentiate into a lamb. That means that embryonic cells can be "harvested" young enough and given by injection to humans.

Realizing this opportunity exists is exciting. However, not enough people know about it. The more people hear and learn about it, the more they will understand it, and with understanding comes approval. It is disturbing to me that there seems to be more concentration on the political ramifications of this treatment rather than the medical breakthrough that it offers. Now, research has proven that stem cells (from animals, from a patient's own bone marrow, or from umbilical cord blood) can heal wounds, and dramatically improve recovery from stroke, heart disease, diabetes, Alzheimer's, multiple sclerosis, and many other illnesses. I am one of the courageous lucky ones who first benefited from this medical miracle before it was fully accepted in the U.S.

It was comforting to know that a team of doctors from around the world flew in regularly to share their knowledge and expertise about this procedure. Even so, before my first injection, I looked up at Dr. A. with concern.

"Are you sure?" I was scared and still had my doubts.

He lowered the syringe to his side and looked at me with compassion, understanding that I needed reassurance.

"Yes, I'm sure," he said confidently.

This became our little ritual. Before each injection, I would ask. "Are you sure?"

He would always answer, "Yes, I am sure."

The day after my first injection, Dr. A asked how I felt. Knowing that the stem cells came from a lamb, I looked up innocently at the doctor and nurses. "Baaaahhh," I uttered.

Everyone was silent until I smiled mischievously, and they realized I was being funny. We all broke into laughter.

Every day I continued to improve. The treatments were working. I could move my hand and arm more freely. And my leg was stronger. In addition to the physical improvements, my mental function dramatically improved. My head felt clearer, almost like a fog was being lifted.

At the end of the first week, Pat and I were invited to have dinner with Cadie and her fiancé at her home. She lived in an apartment building outside the tourist area, so we arranged for a cab to take us. Leaving the heavily guarded village was like entering a different world. Outside on the roads, there were donkeys and small economical cars that were so beaten up they looked like they had come from a demolition derby. I even saw one car without doors. The harsh realties of poverty were all around. Onlookers watched us through the iron gates of their homes as we passed by. It was all I could do not to stare.

Arriving at the apartment building where Cadie lived, we proceeded to enter her home. She asked us to pardon

the confusion, as more than one family shared the small
apartment. The living conditions were unlike anything I
had ever seen. A gas line dangled loose over the kitchen
sink where drinking water boiled in a large tin pot. A
clothesline was strung out the kitchen window with
clothes flapping in the warm island breeze.

Dinner consisted of rice and beans, and for dessert,
Cadie served us canned flan—a delicacy that she had been
saving for a special occasion. As we sat around the living
room we listened to Cadie and her fiancé share stories
about their lives and ambitions. It was heartbreaking for
me to realize that they dreamed of what we in the United
States take for granted: owning a car, having their own
apartment, or just having air-conditioning. They spoke of
the United States as if it were paradise, which made me
realize how fortunate and blessed I was in spite of my
condition.

As the evening drew to a close, darkness filled the room
and the electricity flickered off and on. Cadie lit several
candles almost out of habit and explained how the

government intentionally turned the power off and on throughout the city to punish those who hooked up electricity without paying. Barbaric as this was, she and the others had grown accustomed to the inconvenience and had learned to just ignore it.

When it was time for us to go, Cadie called for another cab. Only the moon and an occasional passing car lit the dark streets as Pat and I sat silently in the backseat of the taxi, pondering the experience we had just shared.

Word of our visit spread at the clinic, and our driver invited us to his home to meet his family. We graciously accepted but explained that we could not stay long.

So after the next day's treatments, Sammy drove us to his home. We were about 30 minutes away when the streets narrowed and we approached a cluster of small wooden homes. There were children playing outside, awaiting our arrival. Parking the van on the street just

Poor housing

outside the front door, Sammy held my arm as I walked with my cane the few steps to the door.

The front door of his humble home was so short we had to lower our heads as we entered. Inside, his entire family greeted us, their smiling faces warm and welcoming. He introduced us to his brothers, sisters, parents, as well as his wife and several children. Seeing their rough living conditions, Pat and I were moved that they were so willing and eager to meet us. Other than Sammy, no one spoke English, so our visit was brief, and full of smiles. What a powerful healing experience that was for me. I'd left the states feeling like a disabled, second-class citizen. But Sammy's gracious family was so honored to have me in their home that I felt like royalty. As we left, my injured self-worth and spirit was lifted.

The week came to an end and Pat had to return home. Like me, she had grown to admire and appreciate the hardworking and gracious people of this beautiful country. Pat and I had shared some memorable times "cutting up" on our strolls through the village and surviving a fierce hurricane together. Her dry sense of humor had kept me smiling, able to see the lighter side of things. I was going to miss having her around. Before leaving, she made arrangements for one of the nurses from the clinic to stay with me.

Mail started to arrive from home. I was anxious to receive word from my family and friends. The cost to make or receive long-distance phone calls was outrageous.

Not that it really mattered; my only real form of communication was writing. The staff noted my strong desire for mail so my nurse took me to an office in the medical plaza and pointed out a fax machine that I could use for a small fee. I was so excited to have a way to communicate with my family and friends back home!

Every day during my first hour of treatment in the *chelation* room, I would prepare faxes to send out in the morning hoping to have a reply by the end of the day. It wasn't long before I was receiving one or more a day. Inspiring and encouraging messages, word of how Alex was doing, and get-well wishes were among the messages I received. My friend, Dr. Spain, from Pensacola, sent me silly jokes and cartoons to make me laugh. Lori, my former workout partner, sent me all kinds of inspirational quotes to keep my spirits up and my mind focused on the big picture. And I received cards from my sisters.

The medical staff and doctors were extremely comforting during my homesickness, but my loneliness was heavy and I longed to be home. Each day I continued to see changes as my body was healing. Going from one treatment room to the next each day, I anxiously looked for improvements.

Supported by therapists on each side of me, I practiced standing and walking on my own. At times they even danced with me to liven things up. The nurses were salsa dancing experts. With or without music, the salsa was in their Latin blood. I had always been a very good dancer, but now I was out of my league. I was doing good just to keep from stepping on their toes. By the second week, I was able to stand on my own and walk without wobbling. Each day I made monumental improvements. I still used my cane, but now I was steady and much more balanced. As the days passed, I could feel my left side gaining strength. A medical miracle was happening right before my eyes.

Dr. Christa, the chief medical director, heard of my remarkable progress and invited me to visit her at her home one weekend. She lived about an hour from the clinic in San Domingo. She insisted I would be safe taking a bus and that she would pick me up upon my arrival. So I was provided a round-trip ticket and boarded the open-air bus that traveled across the island.

It was a clear sunny day, and the sights were both breathtaking and heartbreaking. In contrast with the beautiful countryside that was framed with mountains and blue water, there were thatched homes and dirt yards where children played. The Dominican Republic didn't

seem to have a middle class. The people were either very
well off or incredibly poor. One thing was consistent—
they were very loving and gracious.

When I arrived in San Domingo, Dr. Christa greeted
me as she had promised. She drove me through the city
to the first upper-class residential area I had seen. We
drove through a gated entrance and to her home. From
the third floor balcony, I could see fields of banana trees
with marijuana plants growing between them. Something I
suspected was quite normal for those parts. Among the
plants, I spotted a white rabbit eating the plants. I smiled
wondering how he might feel after eating marijuana all day.

While dinner was being prepared, Dr. Christa gave me a
tour of her lovely home and the guest quarters where her
partner Mr. Freedman lived. He was the engineer who had
designed and built the oxygen chamber for the clinic. I had
seen him through the window of the chamber everyday, but
this was the first time we'd met. Dr. Christa was very nice
and commented on how well my treatments were going.

"I've read in your chart that you were a golfer before
your stroke. Would you like to join us tomorrow morning
for a round of golf at our club?" she asked.

"*Si, muchas gracias,*" I answered. My eyes welled up with
tears, remembering that just months ago, I lay in CCU
dangling between life and death. Returning to the golf
course was a sign for me that I was regaining a normal life.

The next day we all went to the clubhouse for an early
breakfast. Afterward, she drove me around in her golf cart

and gave me a tour of the course. It was unlike anything I had ever seen. Surrounded by mountains and thick tropical foliage, it was a golf course in the middle of a jungle. The clubhouse had no exterior walls and was set on a cliff overlooking the 18th hole. It looked like a Tarzan movie set.

I watched from the golf cart as Dr. Christa and Mr. Freedman teed off, wishing I could be swinging the driver instead. It was all I could do not to grab a 9 iron and punch the next ball. Watching them, I knew it wouldn't be long and I'd be back, swinging with all my determination.

The weekend passed quickly, and I returned to the medical facility to continue my treatments. Day after day, I remained under constant care as I underwent my routine of scheduled treatments.

During my last week, my father flew down for a quick visit. I was looking forward to seeing him. It had been a long time.

My dad is an interesting man. He has a heart of gold when it comes to helping his fellow man, just as long as his fellow man doesn't cross him or get in his way. He is a handsome, well-dressed charmer, with the patience of a gnat. His good heart makes him irresistible to the ladies and easy to forgive, but he packs a punch of prejudice against everything that isn't Caucasian or American. I'm not certain why Dad is that way. Perhaps his father's John Wayne, tough-guy facade had something to do with it.

Pappy would often share stories of driving a tank in
World War II and proudly show off his war wounds. He
might have had a softer side; I just never saw it in the 13
years I knew him before he died.

A natural-born salesman, my dad could sell anything
from property to dreams. His customers warm to his humor
and practical jokes, and many of them become friends. He
has been in so many businesses throughout my lifetime, I
have lost track. Beginning in the banking industry, to
owning a franchise of a major fried-chicken restaurant; to
being a sought-out speaker; he is an all American
businessman. At one time, our living room wall was covered
in awards touting his million-dollar sales accomplishments.

He met the mark in most ways, but was absent in
others. Like many men of his generation, providing for
the family was the priority, rather than being in touch
with the emotional issues. He would join us for church at
Easter and Christmas, but nothing was a sure thing. There
were no set traditions.

During my childhood, he was my hero and I was
Daddy's girl. He would never admit it, but I often felt
like he favored me over my sisters. He and I went fishing
and camping together. He even taught me to shoot a
rifle, skeet shoot with a shotgun, and load buckshot in a
.357 magnum. I became a skilled marksman in no time,
winning shooting contests over the boys. And he taught
me to drive a stick shift before I was 10 years old,
showing me how to work the clutch to climb steep hills.

As I grew up, I admired cars more and more, especially the finer fast ones like Ferraris and Maseratis. Some say I was the son he never had. I was simply a tomboy who loved adventure and thrills. Throughout my childhood, my dad could do no wrong in my eyes. But when I discovered his unfaithfulness to my mom, he quickly fell from his pedestal.

I was still in my teens when my relationship with my dad shifted. He was no longer my idol, but I learned to accept him as he was. I've never questioned his love for me—and I love him very much!

Knowing he was coming to see me was very exciting. Sammy drove me to the airport to pick him up. It was Friday afternoon and my treatments for the week were completed, so we went to the beach. It was the first time I'd been there, and it was more beautiful than I'd imagined. Palm trees lined the beaches, and cabanas were set up for tourists. We sat under a tiki hut and had a cool island beverage while enjoying the sights. Swimsuit tops were optional, and Dad seemed very content with the sunbathers who opted not to wear one! It was a beautiful day and I enjoyed relaxing and being with my father. After a very nice day, he took me to dinner that evening. Our conversation was light. We talked of the weather and his latest girlfriend.

When it was time for him to leave on Sunday morning, I rode along as Sammy drove him to catch his departing flight. I kissed him good-bye and gave him a big hug. As he walked to the small plane that was waiting on the island runway he turned and waved.

"I love you, 'B,'" he shouted. "B" is the nickname he gave me as a little girl, and he has called me that ever since. He turned and boarded the plane.

On the way back from the airport, I wondered why we had never discussed why he hadn't come to see me while I was in the hospital. I suppose it was a wound neither of us wanted to open.

While it serves as no excuse, over the years, I came to learn that when my dad was faced with the thought of me dying, he went into denial rather than running to be by my side. Sadly, at the time, this only made me feel more abandoned. Neither my mother nor father was present during the most critical time of my life. For many years, this was, and still can be, hard to even think about. Then a very good therapist advised me to write about my feelings, expressing how deeply this had hurt me.

"Even if you never share these letters with your parents, writing your feelings will help you release the anger and hurt," she advised me. It took years of therapy before I began to heal and learn to forgive them.

My last weekend at the clinic finally arrived, and my sister Angie flew down to escort me home. She was accompanied by our mutual friend Bonnie whom I was excited to see. Bartering with one of the locals, I arranged for a horse-drawn carriage to pick them up at the hotel in the morning and bring them to the clinic.

Bonnie and Angie in horse-drawn carriage

That evening my doctor made reservations at a special restaurant that was notorious for its unique location—in a huge tree. It sat high above the ground with lions and exotic animals on display in cages beneath. A large table was waiting for us, and after everyone was seated, they toasted my recovery and congratulated me on all my hard work. While I still had much more physical therapy ahead of me to fine-tune my recovery, the treatment had been very successful. Angie and Bonnie enjoyed the rest of the evening with me cutting up and pretending to smoke the expensive cigars that were given to everyone after dinner. We even ventured down to the lion's den for a closer look.

The remainder of the weekend we prepared for our return home. Angie and Bonnie shopped for souvenirs, while I gathered mementos and gifts for the staff.

Once again I had bonded with a group of special

people and knew I would miss them. They had all been instrumental in my survival and hold a special place in my heart and memories forever!

CHAPTER EIGHT

A New Beginning

I'd worked diligently at my recovery, hoping to return to my former career and my former life. But my stroke had insured that I wouldn't be able to go back. I would have to find a way to move me forward.

October 1996

It wasn't long after I returned home that I realized that even though my treatments at the clinic had restored much of my function, I would not be able to return to the work I had been doing. I was grateful that I no longer needed the wheelchair but I still had to rely on my cane for support, and I walked slowly and with a severe limp. My cane was unlike any you'd find in the rehab center or supply store. It was custom-made out of mahogany, with

an antique glass doorknob for a handle. I figured that as
long as I had to use a cane, it was going to be a pretty one.

My physical challenges were still great, and my speech was
slurred and hard to understand. It would take four more
years of speech therapy before I could be easily understood.
Even then, my speech impairment was only a small part of
the challenges that would keep me from resuming my career.
The biggest challenge was that I was unable to add and
subtract money accurately. Calculating million-dollar estate
cases for my wealthy clients was no longer possible. I was
doing good to figure up small purchases and transactions.
Whenever I bought groceries or my medication, I became
nervous, uncertain if I had enough money to cover my
purchase. I would hand the clerk a $20 or $50, hoping it
was enough to cover everything and trusting that I would be
given correct change. Once, when I handed the grocery clerk
a $20, she looked at me strangely.

"It's $21.98. You are short $1.98."

I froze, not knowing what to do. The idea of putting
something back did not occur to me. After a long pause,
she could tell something was wrong and so could the
people waiting in line. A very kind person behind me gave
the clerk two dollars, and I left the store humiliated and
embarrassed.

I was obviously challenged in math and would have a
hard time returning to work, especially in the financial
arena. My only income was from my disability insurance,
and that just covered the house payment and electric bill.

I adored my beautiful home—it was the first house I'd ever called my own. I'd had my eye on it for years before it became available for lease-purchase. The interior designer who'd remodeled it had decided to move, just as I was looking to buy. It was perfect timing. Realizing now that I could no longer afford to keep it was a harsh revelation. Without the income from my career, there was no way I could maintain the standard of living to which I'd grown accustomed. So the house was put on the market and sold within a week to the first person to look at it.

As soon as the house sold, I mailed out flyers announcing that I was having an estate sale. My life as I knew it was over, and I was forced to let go and start over with almost nothing.

It was October, and one of my favorite times, Halloween, was just around the corner. I wanted to have one last party in my home. So, I asked two friends if they would help me arrange a Halloween party. I couldn't speak well enough to be understood over the phone, so they agreed to invite the guests and arrange for the food. I had so much fun decorating the house. Within a few days, the house resembled a haunted mansion. On Halloween night, the front yard was covered with tombstones, spider webs hung from the porch, and the bedroom curtains on the second floor blew out from the windows, with a strobe light intermittently lighting up the room. A soundtrack of eerie organ music drifted out of the house and misty fog, created with dry ice, floated along the ground. It was spooky—and so was I, dressed in a gory monster mask.

As the party guests arrived, I sat quietly on the front porch swing, holding a bucket of candy and awaiting any last trick-or-treaters.

Some of the arriving guests were women I'd not met. They'd been invited by my friends. One woman, Missy, took the time to have a conversation with me, really listening so she could understand what I was saying. I learned that she was on partial disability because of her *fibromyalgia*. We hit it off right away and became good friends. Besides having physical challenges in common, we both cracked each other up with the silliest things. Sometimes all we had to do was look at each other, and we'd bust out laughing.

Missy was incredibly supportive, even offering to help at the estate sale the next weekend. That Saturday, I sold most everything in the house that I couldn't fit in my car or a small U-Haul. My beautiful furniture, china, and antiques were all sold. And, everything was priced to sell quickly. I didn't want to do this twice. I watched as people carried away my patio furniture, my Bose sound system and TV, and even my expensive business suits and pumps.

One buyer asked if my speed skates were for sale. What once was a prized possession was now becoming extinct, replaced by in-line skates. So many fond memories were held in those skates. I was the fastest backward speed skater at the rink. Every Friday night I lined up with six

other tough girls to race to the finish for a 25-cent
Slurpie.

"Sure," I said to the buyer. "$10 and they are yours."

Letting go of everything was tough, but selling my 12-
string guitar was the toughest. I'd been writing songs and
playing the guitar since I was 8 years old. I had taken
private lessons from one of the best guitar players around.
I'd first heard him play while dining at a fine restaurant
with my dad one night. He could play like Chet Atkins,
and I was fascinated with his skill. Dad inquired if he
taught, and he did, so my first lesson was arranged. My
mom and dad both came along.

"Teach her to play the theme song to *Dr. Zhivago,*" my
dad requested.

"And teach her to play 'Amazing Grace,'" my mother
insisted.

I eventually learned both, but it was "Amazing Grace" that I
was expected to play and sing, at my parents' Christmas parties
and Amway meetings—not my idea of fun.

It didn't take long before my guitar teacher discovered
that I could play by ear, and he began switching the sheet
music constantly to force me to identify the notes. I
practiced daily, causing my fingers to bleed and eventually
form calluses. Over the years my guitar became more than
a musical instrument—it became a means of expressing
what I felt inside. Selling it was not easy for me.

Fortunately, my best friend from high school bought it
for her husband.

When the estate sale was finally over, and everyone was gone, I sat on the hardwood floor in my empty house and cried. Grief overwhelmed me. All evidence of my former successful life was gone. All I had left were a dozen boxes of clothes and keepsakes. I had no idea what the future held for me.

It was a good thing that my friend Cindy in Seattle, Washington, had invited me out to stay for a few months. She was retiring and was anxious to show me the great Northwest. So I packed my camera and warm clothes, and Alex and I boarded a flight. As we flew into Seattle, I looked out the small window to see the top of Mount Rainer breaking through the clouds. The pilot announced that Rainer was one of the highest mountains in the world and the top of it remained covered in snow year-round. Already, the change of scenery was healing my broken spirit.

Cindy picked me up at the airport, chatting excitedly about the trips she'd planned. Being a photographer, I was anxious to capture some of the world's most-photographed sites. Our first adventure was driving up Mount Rainer to a lookout tower at the top. We drove past fields of tulips, cherry farms, and majestic waterfalls. I spotted deer, wild ponies, and even cute little chipmunks—rare sights for a Florida girl! As we continued up Rainer, the temperature dropped dramatically. Snow covered the ground, and icicles hung from the walls of rock that lined the road. Soon we were surrounded by snow. We kept driving upward, through white misty clouds, and finally our view cleared and we were able to look down. We were above the clouds! I felt like a bird soaring to new heights.

After a long day of sight-seeing, we returned down the mountain to Cindy's Seattle home, to plan our next destination. This was fun. Cindy was a great tour guide and very caring about my challenges. She always carried my camera gear and made sure I was comfortable and warm.

Our next stop was the old mining town where the sitcom *Northern Exposure* was filmed. Just as the show depicted, it was a one-stoplight town with a corner bar and a couple of cafés. I think the graveyard was the most startling and historic sight. It was unlike any cemetery I'd ever seen: Old tombstones, dating back to the 1800s, sat crooked, scattered over a rough, uneven hilltop. The locals shared that many of those buried there had died in the mines. Their resting places offered a reminder of their poor economic status.

It was late and we'd been driving all day, so we stopped for the night at a mountain inn. As we pulled in the parking lot, I started laughing at a tall statue of a hairy black bear-like thing that was standing in the driveway.

"What's with the weird bear?" I asked.

Laughing, Cindy quickly informed me that it was a statue of Bigfoot, who was a very real phenomenon to the people there.

The next morning, we had breakfast in a little diner and headed out to see Mount St. Helens. Along the way, we stopped at a tourist center and watched a movie about the earthquake that awakened the sleeping volcano in 1980, 16 years earlier. This famous volcano caused massive destruction that could be seen two states away. Two hundred thirty-square miles of thick old-growth forest were blown away. The mudflows scoured another 100 miles. For over a month following the eruption, the sky was dark as ashes fell over Washington and neighboring states.

As we approached the mountain, trees lay on their sides like thousands of toothpicks that had been pushed over. Riverbeds sat empty, parched and cracked where water once rushed. As we drove up a nearby ridge, Cindy pulled into an overlook parking area and we got out of the car.

We walked over to the edge to look out over the eruption site. It was a perfect spot for a photograph, but all I could do was stare. Studying the destruction that went for miles and miles, I tried to comprehend the force of the blast that caused such devastation. As I stared at the barren land that was covered with the carcasses of dead trees, I began to notice patches of green new growth. The mountain was still alive; deep inside were seeds that survived the heat and mud, and they had sprouted and were growing. Seedlings and shrubs had taken root, filling in the spaces where their ancestors had stood proudly.

The land now had a very serene, spiritual energy. As I sat there, I realized that my life was similar to this mountain in many ways. We had both been tried by fire, forced to find strength from deep within.

After a few months of traveling with Cindy, I was ready to return to Florida to resume therapy. My dad had invited me to live with him in his condo on the beach near Pensacola, Florida. Fortunately, there was a well-known rehabilitation center just down the street. So I had my boxes and my car shipped to his address, and I flew down to live with my Dad.

Alex and my 300ZX were my two "babies." I loved my car. I bought it right after high school through an ad in the paper. When I called the number listed, the owner insisted that I'd have to see it to believe it. She lived in a very nice mobile home park with garages and paved driveways. Arriving at her home, I knocked at the door. She answered looking like she just stepped out of Mel's dinner. Dressed in her apron and a paper tiara pinned to her beehive hairdo, she explained that she didn't drive the car for fear it might get hit or messed up. Tears came to her eyes as she explained that she was forced to sell the car in order to qualify for her new home. Garaged, it was in showroom condition, plastic covers still on the backseat. It was just what I wanted; I kept it for 14 years while all my friends drove their BMWs and Mercedes.

"Sell that rice rocket," they'd all say.

"Think what you want," I'd tell them. "My car is beautiful and fast." I loved taking the T-tops off and driving to the beach. It became a collector's item after Nissan stopped making them in 1997.

Now, with my weak left leg, it was tough to work the clutch, but I was determined to drive. You'd have to pry my cold fingers off the gear shift before telling me I couldn't drive it. I was a die-hard sports car enthusiast— and stubborn! Fortunately, Gulf Breeze was a tiny island town and didn't have much traffic.

Living on the beach might sound like a vacation, but it wasn't for me. At least three days a week, sometimes more, I'd go to the rehab center, for my physical, occupational, and speech therapy. Other than this, my time was spent alone. My dad traveled a lot. He tried to be home on the weekends, but his business did not always allow him that luxury. At times my loneliness was so heavy I could feel it. Sitting on the back porch, day after day, I would watch the ocean waves crash onto the sandy white beach, wishing I could be riding one of the passing Waverunners. As night fell, I'd watch the lights from passing ships until they faded into the horizon.

Occasionally, I'd wander through some shops or have lunch at a café, but when you dine alone it doesn't take very long. And, interacting in public was often uncomfortable and humiliating for me. People reacted normally to me—until I started talking. Hearing me slur, many assumed I was drunk and would ignore or avoid me. Others assumed I was mentally challenged and would talk slower and louder. My dad's condo became my hideaway of solitude, where I journalized my experiences, hoping that one day someone would read them and understand what a stroke survivor goes through.

I had seen the neighbors in the next unit, an attractive couple about my age. They had been returning home one evening at the same time the pizza guy was delivering my dinner. I smiled at them as they opened their door, but did not speak. I didn't want them wondering what was wrong with me.

One day after rehab I was sitting on the dock in the back of the condos when they came out to check their crab cages. The handsome man extended his hand to shake mine.

"Hi, my name is Kevin and this is my wife Kathleen. We live in the unit next to you. I know you've been here a while, and I'm sorry we haven't met sooner. We know your dad and he mentioned you might be coming to live with him."

I guess my dad must have told him about my stroke, because they didn't look surprised when I spoke. They were extremely kind and genuinely compassionate about my condition. We sat on the dock for an hour talking. Having their company was wonderful. As the daylight faded, the Florida mosquitoes came out for dinner, prompting us to gather our things and proceed indoors.

Kathleen extended a dinner invitation that I gladly accepted. This was the beginning of a long friendship. We dined together often and talked and talked. Some nights we'd just watch movies or play a board game. Whatever we did, I felt like part of their family and grew to love them.

My stroke had reduced the number of people whom I called friends. But the quality of those friends made up for the loss. Kevin and Kathleen helped me overcome my inhibitions about speaking and going out in public. They helped me realize that once people understood the reason for my challenges, their attitude would change and they would warm up to me. Andy called frequently to check on me along with a few others. And, Rhonna, a high school friend wrote to me often offering compassion, loyalty, and love. Over the years, she never forgot my birthday and was always willing to lend a shoulder to cry on when I'd suffer a heartbreak.

Andy's job had him traveling through North Florida, and he often stopped for a visit. During one visit, he stayed over the weekend, and we planned a day of canoeing. After an early-morning breakfast at the Waffle House, we headed for the river about an hour's drive away. Before we turned off the expressway onto a long winding country road, we stopped at Stuckey's to buy some snacks. As we stood at the cash register to pay, I glanced at the items for sale at the counter. I noticed a fake Elvis driver's license. Laughing, I bought one as a gag gift for Andy.

After renting the canoe, we started out. It was a cool fall day. Andy paddled while I photographed the sites. The crystal-clear shallow water was bordered by large white sand dunes that framed the path of the river. The trees were thick and it was so quiet that we could hear the wind blowing through the leaves. It felt good to be

outdoors and behind the lens of my camera again. Most of
the river was shallow, except for an occasional deep spot.
This was comforting to me, as I was unable to swim.

The half-day trip had gone by quickly and the end was
in sight. Suddenly, as we turned the last bend, the current
picked up and we hit a log, losing control. Instantly the
canoe overturned, in the deepest part of the river! Andy
and I and everything we had in the canoe were dumped
into the current. As we fell in, I glanced around for help.
Unbelievably, two men stood on the bank, watching us.

Stunned by the freezing cold water, clawing to keep
afloat in my heavy clothes, I yelled to Andy.

"My camera! My camera! Please get my camera!" The
camera bag was still wrapped around me, but my treasured
Nikon camera and lenses had fallen into the dark depths.
As soon as Andy made sure that I was safely holding onto
the capsized canoe, he dove for the camera. I looked up to
see if the men on the shore were going to assist us. But they
made no effort to help us or rescue our belongings.

As Andy came up for air, one of the men yelled out,
"Thar' goes your hat," pointing to cap that Andy had
been wearing. Andy continued his search for my camera.
Diving into the cold waters again, he resurfaced, this time
with the camera. I then realized that my lens was gone.

"Andy, the lens! The lens! Please, can you go back
down and find my lens?" Andy dove back down into the
dark water, feeling for the lens. He resurfaced, this time
with my lens!

I looked at the men on the nearby shore, wondering if they would come help us, my cold lips shivering trying to form the words to ask. Instead, they both just watched, entertained, as they pointed at our belongings floating past them.

Grateful for Andy, I clung to him as he swam me to shore. I climbed up onto the bank, shivering, teeth chattering, clothes dripping, and watched the tobacco-chewing men, who were still pointing out our items floating down river.

Andy dragged the canoe to the rental rack and we hurried to the truck, wet and cold. All I could think about was my camera.

"Andy, we have to find a camera shop." It was almost 5 p.m., and many of the stores in the small town were closing. "I know where there is one; we've got to get to it!" Andy drove quickly to the camera shop. When we arrived, I rushed into the small store.

"My camera's soaked!" I held it up to the elderly man behind the counter like a worried mother handing her sick child to a doctor. "Can you save it?"

Realizing the urgency, the man grabbed the camera and without a word to me, ran into the back room. Andy had joined me and we stood shivering, our wet clothes dripping on the old linoleum floor. About 30 minutes later, the man returned from the back room.

"Your camera and lens are going to be fine," he said. "You got here just in time. I took them apart and put them into a special dryer. You can pick them up tomorrow."

Back in the car, grateful to be OK, Andy and I began to laugh about the incident. Suddenly, I remembered the Elvis driver's license. I reached in the back pocket of my still-wet jeans, but it was gone. It must have floated down the river with all our other stuff. I started laughing hysterically.

"What's so funny?," Andy asked.

It was several minutes before I could stop laughing long enough to share the image in my mind of a couple of redneck fishermen, like the men on the shore today, who might find the license floating by, retrieve it and attest that they had proof that, "Elvis *is* alive!"

The eventful day had ended well, even for my camera. Nearly drowning made me think. I realized then that I needed more therapy to relearn to swim, especially before I would go boating again.

A year had passed since I'd come to my dad's beach condo, and all the rigorous therapy had paid off. My speech was improving. My leg and arm moved more fluidly. Even though I was self-conscious of my speech impairment and my limp, I had come a very long way. I was healing, physically and emotionally.

CHAPTER NINE

Justice Unveiled

A "Letter of Intent" to pursue litigation was filed in 1997, marking the beginning of a long, difficult legal battle, which lasted for nearly five years.

During the year following my stroke, friends within the medical and legal community insisted that an investigation was warranted. There were too many unanswered questions. Why had I not been started on a blood thinner sooner than 36 hours after my arrival to the emergency room? Why were my overwhelmingly obvious symptoms of a stroke taken so lightly and overlooked?

While I do not believe in the frivolous lawsuits that seem to plague our country, I do believe that when mistakes are made, especially ones that significantly injure a person, there should be accountability. After lengthy consultations with medical and legal professionals and a lot of soul-searching, I reached the decision to pursue litigation. I knew that it might be a long, costly, and perhaps a disappointing experience. But, that didn't matter; this was about principle.

Friends within the legal community began calling malpractice law firms, asking for support. Some law firms replied that they could not represent me due to conflicts; others came to my home to hear my story. I learned that while my case had enormous potential, it also had enormous risks and costs. Only a few local firms had the resources and the willingness to sue such a large corporation. Night after night I lay awake wondering if I should just let go and let God have His justice. But something inside me kept encouraging me to keep going.

I remembered the story of David and Goliath in the Bible—about a young boy who slays a giant with only a slingshot. I felt like David standing before the giant.

Several months passed and I received a phone call from a doctor I knew. He gave me the name of a lawyer that he'd spoken to about my situation who was willing to review my case. So once again I set out to tell my story.

Entering the lawyer's office nestled in Orlando's downtown historic district, I waited patiently in the lobby. His personal assistant introduced herself and escorted me to the conference room. I waited a few moments for the lawyer to come in. He was tan, with blond hair and blue eyes, and dressed like a *GQ* model. I felt like I was in an episode of *L.A. Law*!

After we exchanged questions and information for several hours, he agreed to take my case. From what I had gathered, his specialty was large malpractice cases. I appreciated his willingness to take my case. His assistant brought in contracts for me to sign, and by the end of the day, I was fully represented.

I learned it would take two years to investigate and prepare my case—maybe longer. It would be an excruciating test of patience. Fortunately, I'd had many lessons in patience recovering from my stroke.

During this time, I continued full-time therapy. Every day, I rode my stationary bike and walked on a treadmill. At times, I was so anxious to run I would increase the speed of the treadmill when my therapist wasn't watching. To my disappointment, my weak knee would buckle, and I'd collapse.

Since I was the youngest stroke survivor in rehab, I found myself always trying to lighten things up with humor. I'd ask who was ready to race me on the stationary bike or announce that everyone was invited to my place for bungee jumping with me after class. I just loved making the older patients smile and laugh. Too many of them were overwhelmed with despair. I was always looking for someone to laugh at my practical jokes anyway. And, you could say, I had a captive audience. For me, rehab was a safe haven where my limitations could be understood, and I didn't feel different.

Inside the rehab room, filled with colored therapy balls and weights, we had the privilege to ask one another questions that might be considered prying or even rude in the "outside world." When it came my turn to share my experience, I'd explain how I had suffered a massive stroke at the age of 31. My older friends would sigh and shake their heads, sad that I'd experienced such a horrific thing at such a young age.

I'll never forget the time I sat in the handicapped section at a professional baseball game. The entire row was filled mostly with elderly people in wheelchairs who looked at me and my friend in astonishment.

"Why is *she* sitting here?" I could almost hear them wondering.

I told my friend that I would be a minute as I had some "politicking" to do. I leaned over and quietly said to a woman sitting next to me that I would love to sit closer to the ball field but because of my injury I was unable to manage the stairs.

"Well, honey, what *is* your injury?" she asked.

Sharing that I'd survived a massive stroke years prior, I explained that at one time I was completely paralyzed on my entire left side. This launched her into reporter mode, and like wild fire, news of my condition spread quickly all the way down the row. Within minutes, strangers were asking me questions and sharing their survivor stories.

I turned back to my friend and smiled.

"Well, I'm in."

Times like these helped me to realize that I had been given a gift that I had to share with others. After talking with so many survivors from all types of injuries and conditions, I could see that my experience inspired and touched lives. More importantly, it gave hope. Sharing my story with the world became my motivation to keep getting better. So, I continued typing away, keeping track of my experiences. Nearly every day, I'd peck at my keyboard one-handed.

For the next couple of years I continued physical therapy, as I stayed engrossed in my legal case. Working on my case stimulated me; it helped me to focus on something other than word games and leg presses. I was eager to see the case through and have justice served. I had always enjoyed law, never imagining I'd find myself relying on it so intently.

Danny, one of the young lawyers working on my case was assigned to the gathering of evidence and expert depositions. He was tall, handsome, and extremely bright. We became friends, and he taught me a lot about law, particularly malpractice law. I came to appreciate that, while my case had overwhelming evidence of negligence and damages, it was challenged by causation. In layman terms, this meant that as the plaintiff, I had the "burden of proof" to demonstrate that there was at least a 50% medical certainty that if I had been started on a blood

thinner when I arrived in the emergency room—instead
of 36 hours later—it would have changed my outcome.
Although common sense dictates that it most likely would
have, it still had to be presented as a medical certainty
based on statistics and studies done from medical
research. Unfortunately, because I was so unusually young
to have a stroke, and a female, there were no studies
available.

Over time as I worked with Danny and other lawyers,
I came to learn that a fierce animosity existed between my
lawyer and the opposing counsel. Rather than sharing a
professional respect for one another, it was rumored that
they despised one another. This was brought to my
attention one day during a hearing I attended in the
judge's chamber. The judge reprimanded my lawyer for
keeping a letter that was inadvertently sent to him. My
impression was that my lawyer had ignored the request to
return it and had allowed it to be seen by other parties.
This only fueled the flames that had been burning for
some time between the lawyers.

In the end, I was the one to suffer as several delays and
undue hardships were, ironically, placed on my case. I was
caught in a battle between angry lawyers, resulting in
unnecessary delays and expenses. My costs were already
approaching a quarter of a million dollars and the case
had not yet seen a courtroom. At this point, it had now
been nearly four years of the case being delayed and
rescheduled.

I knew the time had come to seek new representation. I was unsure who would take my case at such a late stage or where I could even begin to look. But I knew something had to change.

My first thought was to look for a co-counselor. I learned that this option was within my legal rights, but would have to be approved by my lawyer. One day I picked up a magazine whose headline read "The Most Feared Lawyer in Florida." The cover photo showed a kind but powerful-looking face. I turned to the article and read about this respected attorney in Palm Beach, only a few hours from Orlando. Maybe he was the one who could help me. I wrote him a letter, outlining my case, and asking if he would represent me as co-counsel.

A week later I followed up with a phone call and left a message with his personal assistant. Days passed and I began to doubt that he would call me. I worried that a lawyer of his stature wouldn't accept a position as co-counsel so late in a case. The next day, the phone rang, and when I looked at the caller ID, I saw his firm's name across the screen.

"YES!" I said, and then calmly answered the phone. He was very nice, offering his condolences about my stroke and the difficulties of my legal pursuit. He was brief, saying that while he usually does not co-counsel cases, he had considered my situation and would like to help me. His only condition was that my lawyer had to agree to it.

That afternoon I faxed a memo to my lawyer, outlining my request. But my request was ignored, even after several inquiries.

I prayed for wisdom and guidance to know how to proceed. Later that week, when I went for my manicure my answer came. For 35 years, Ena's nail salon has been one of the best little networking spots in town. What makes Ena so special is her caring and thoughtfulness. During my years on disability, she gave me a full manicure for half of her going rate. She wanted me to feel nurtured and loved. Her Winter Park salon attracted prestigious business people ranging from senators to vacationing CEOs. Whenever she felt that one of them might be able to help me, she would introduce us, briefly explaining my story.

When I arrived for my appointment, Ena was excited for me to meet Fran, a client and successful businesswoman. Fran heard my story and recommended that I retain a personal legal consultant to manage my situation. I had never heard of a personal legal consultant, but after hearing her experience, I took the name and number of one she recommended.

I called his office the next day and scheduled an appointment. After reviewing my circumstances, he agreed to write a letter to my lawyer. Within a week of his letter, my co-counsel request was arranged and the Palm Beach lawyer flew to Orlando, prepared for mediation.

Mediation is a formal meeting between opposing parties and their lawyers for the purpose of attempting to reach a settlement before going to trial. My mediation began with the opposing lawyers requesting that my out-of-town co-counselor withdraw his representation.

"I will not be withdrawing from the case—and I'm offended by the request," he firmly replied.

The mediation lasted all day and into the early evening. I was exhausted. By 6 p.m., an agreement had not been reached. I was told that this might be due to the hostilities that were still brewing over the letter my lawyer had not returned. This was the last straw. I was not going to allow what seemed like a personal vendetta to jeopardize my case. I had come too far and fought too hard.

Totally frustrated, I scheduled a session with my psychologist, Dr. Anne Diebel, the next day. Since my stroke, she had been a source of wisdom and support for me. A professor to many leading therapists, she had been recommended by one of my doctors as being highly distinguished in her field. She was wise, compassionate, and genuinely cared about me. She had become my mentor and friend.

In our session, I explained what had happened during the mediation and that I felt that my case was being jeopardized and that I couldn't handle much more. She knew that I had reached the point of exhaustion and was greatly concerned that the intense stress could endanger my life by triggering another stroke. A resolution had to be reached soon. That evening, she made a phone call to a prominent lawyer who had been her friend for years. Highly respected within the legal community, Michael Maher was a former president of the American Trial Lawyers Association. The next day, when Dr. Diebel called to tell me she had arranged for me to meet with him, I was ecstatic!

Once again, I found myself in a legal office telling my story to a lawyer. I shared the facts of my case and the events that had transpired over the last four years while trying to resolve it. At times I cried; other times we laughed. He was very kind and sincere. At the conclusion of our meeting, he assured me that the transition to his firm's representation would not be difficult, as he had known my current lawyer since he was a boy. He also added that he and my co-counselor were very close friends.

So I wrote my lawyer and relinquished his representation.

Signing contacts with the new firm, I sighed with relief. A heavy burden had been lifted, and, almost immediately, everything started turning around. My message to the opposition was clear: I was not going away. Within the next few weeks, my trial was scheduled and a new mediation was set.

Dressed in one of my finest suits, I arrived at the firm early and was seated in one of the rooms set up for all the separate defendants—each with their lawyers and insurance adjusters. A mediator went around to each room to discuss each party's position and argument, and then return to my lawyers to negotiate. This went on for three days as we rapidly approached my trial date.

On the fourth day, we were exchanging offers via long-distance phone calls. My lawyers were now encouraging me to settle.

"It is not worth the risk of losing everything," my lawyer said. "Even if a jury awards you a verdict, an appeal will probably be filed by the defendants, which could take another two years."

Mr. Maher had become like a father to me. I trusted him and his impeccable legal experience to guide me.

I drove to a nearby park and took my shoes off and walked around. I was "grounding" myself as I pondered and prayed for wisdom.

"Is this what I should do?" I asked God.

I was grateful for the offer made, but I just wasn't sure what to do.

Then, like a feather floating down from heaven, my answer came. The words I'd so often heard my Grandmother say to me rang through, "*Peace. Be still.*" I'm sure she was watching over me, especially that day, embracing me with her great faith and helping me to see the power of letting go. A peace came over me, assuring me that God would always take care of me.

Calling my lawyer who was in New York at the time, I agreed to settle for the last offer submitted.

After nearly five long years, my fight for accountability and justice was finally settled.

CHAPTER TEN

Letting Go

In order to create a new life, we must let go
of the old. My stroke forced me to learn to
let go. I'd already released the life I'd
planned. Now I was learning to release
attachment to outcomes and to others'
approval. The hardest was letting go
of loved ones.

With the help of family, friends, and some wonderful
therapists, I made remarkable progress during the first few
years following my stroke. But, sitting up alone night after
night, I longed for companionship and love outside my
circle of support. And because my sexual orientation is
different, my search was even more challenging. While I
always admired my male friends and high school
boyfriends, I never had a physical attraction or felt the

"warm fuzzies" that my sisters and girlfriends would experience when guys were around. For many years, I felt as though I was deprived of what seemed to be everyone's expectations of normal. My heritage was that of a proper Southern girl: You married, had children, and went to church on Sundays. No one demonstrated this more gracefully than my beautiful grandmother. Always wearing white gloves to church and waiting for doors to be opened by a gentleman, she was a true Southern lady. A hat model and a self-educated woman, she was well versed in many subjects, and she treasured the books that taught her. She showed me how to garden, to can pears, and to have impeccable manners.

Fun abounded throughout my childhood, as the neighborhood boys and I found similar interests—rolling nickels, trading pocketknives, and building tree forts. But, as I grew into a woman, these tomboy interests quickly faded. During my high school years, I dated several guys just because it seemed like the thing to do. I was escorted to my prom by a very handsome male model. Within a few years, I received a marriage proposal from a wealthy man whom I met in the business world.

I had choices; being gay wasn't one of them. It wasn't until my early twenties that I told my family I had been in a committed relationship for seven years and loved "her" dearly. I'm not sure exactly what they thought, but I know they never really accepted it, especially my mom. She believed that if she accepted me she would be approving my lifestyle—and that went against everything she believed. Her pastor encouraged her to disassociate from me so I might see the error of my ways and come "home." She decided to ban me from her life and home in hopes that it would force me to change. This hurt me deeply. She often compared her decision to the story in the Bible of the prodigal son—a story about a boy who went into the world to live sinfully while his parents lovingly awaited his return. I wanted her acceptance so much that I tried going on a few dates with men in order to make her happy, but I was miserable.

The more I tried to be who I wasn't, the easier it became to let go of my fears and accept that I was gay. I'm not always proud of the way the gay community is represented, but I learned that much of what is portrayed is skewed and limited to certain groups. Every community has extremes and rough edges that we could judge as bad or wrong—until we take the time to get to know people and try to understand them.

January 1976

I had learned this lesson early in life. I had been an honor student throughout Christian and prep school up until the middle of sixth grade. It was during the late seventies when my parents were contemplating their first divorce. My dad seemed eager to consent to most of my requests, so when I asked if I could enter public school, he said, "Sure 'B', whatever you want." My mother was unhappy with his decision, as it went against her desires for schooling in a Christian environment.

My first day of public school, I waited nervously at the
bus stop. Grateful that I didn't have to wear a uniform
and wanting to look my best, I'd selected a preppy blazer
and pants to wear, along with my fur-lined jacket since it
was cold. Big mistake! My neighborhood was the first bus
stop, and when the large yellow bus arrived, I boarded it
and made my way to a seat in the back. In private school,
I'd been picked up every morning by a van at the edge of
my driveway. It was customary to allow the older students
to sit up front where the air-conditioning was the coolest.
Little did I know that the back of the bus was reserved for
the oldest and toughest kids.

As the bus made several stops, I was surprised how
many of the kids stayed near the front. At the last stop, a
group of tough-looking girls boarded the bus and headed
straight for the back.

"Who are *you?*" the biggest girl asked, "And what are
you doing in my seat?"

I immediately offered to move, but before I could, they
surrounded me and grabbed my lunch bag.

"What do you have in here?" one girl asked as she opened
the bag. "Let's see: a tuna sandwich, an apple, and, look—a
note from mommy! Isn't that sweet? Do you like apples?"

I nodded, and before I could predict her next action, she
shoved the apple into my mouth. As I pried it loose from my
teeth, I stood up to move. But the group of girls stood over me,
having fun at my expense. All the way to school, they picked on
me, making fun of my fur-lined coat and preppy outfit.

The bus driver, hearing the altercation, yelled over her shoulder, "Keep it quiet back there!"

When I got off the bus, the principal saw that I had been roughed up and asked me to come into his office.

"Who did this to you?" he demanded.

"I don't know them," I replied. "It's my first day here."

He called my parents, and my dad came to pick me up. When he arrived, he and the principal agreed that the girls should be punished. But retribution was not how I wanted to solve this problem. I refused to describe the girls. As soon as I got home, I cut the sleeves off my new jean jacket and frayed the edges. Then I took it to my mom and asked her to sew "Val" on the back.

The next day, dressed in jeans, a T-shirt, and my rough-looking blue jean jacket, I boarded the bus and made my way to a seat just two rows from the back. I knew I was risking a second altercation, but I was determined not to let those girls start off my public school experience thinking they could abuse me. When they got on, a hush fell over the noisy bus. We stared at each other as they slowly walked to the back, where I was seated.

Standing over me again, the biggest girl spoke, "Hi, my name is Joannie. Sorry about yesterday. You looked so funny we couldn't help ourselves. Thanks for not squealing on us."

I instantly became part of the popular group at school. Joannie and the other girls were not so tough after all. They were just acting from a place of self-preservation, trying to protect themselves from being hurt or unaccepted. They were always looking out for me—showing me the ropes of public school—whose class was the easiest to skip, where to hide if the bell rang before you made class, and which teachers to avoid.

I enjoyed running track, and signed up for the track team, making friends with the other "jocks." At practices, Joannie and her group would sit on the embankment of the track, smoking, and yell, "Go Val!" as I ran like the wind. Smoking was very popular in the seventies, especially in certain circles, even at such an early age. Fortunately, my coach wanted everyone on the track team to understand the negative effects of smoking, so he arranged for two sets of lungs to be brought to the science lab. One was black and sticky, looking like they had been burned. The other was soft and pink. That visual lesson kept me from ever smoking. The girls respected my decision and admired my commitment, even though they continued to puff like smokestacks.

Joannie and the girls were definitely rough around the edges, but they were surviving their own challenges just as I was.

Fall 1978

By ninth grade, we went on to high school together—all, except for Joannie. A few weeks before the summer was over, she was killed in a car wreck on the way home from the skating rink. For the first time, I became brutally aware of the harsh realities of life and how quickly it can change.

Looking back, I see how many extraordinary lessons were woven into the fabric of my childhood, preparing me for my own challenging future.

Growing up in a turbulent household, I was grateful for the calming influence of my grandmother. When I was little, she would read to me as she rocked me to sleep. The book she read most often was from the Berenstain Bears series, the one in which the father bear gives his son a new bike. While the father demonstrates how to ride it, the little bear watches his father make many mistakes, barely escaping disaster. Never admitting his obvious blunders, the father bear says, "*Now let that be a lesson to you.*" In the end, the little bear acknowledges his father as a great teacher who shows him what *not* to do.

My grandmother saved this precious book in plastic wrap and gave it to me when I was in my twenties. By that time, I could see the deeper meaning in the story. We all come to learn our own lessons, but, if we are wise, we can choose to learn from the experience of others. I keep the storybook in a box of treasured memorabilia; I keep the lesson in my heart.

1999

Three years after my stroke, I finally felt that my life was in balance. I was seeing a woman I loved, I looked and felt great, and my lawsuit was finally nearing conclusion.

Unfortunately, the woman I was seeing was going through some difficult times. Distraught over several personal losses, she became depressed and dependent on prescription drugs. I grew deeply concerned as she threatened to take her life. I even arranged for her to be seen at a clinic for depression and drug abuse. Unfortunately, her appointment was a few weeks away.

I'll never know if treatment could have helped her. She was drunk one night when she called me at 2 a.m. asking me to care for her dog should anything happen to her. As soon as I agreed, a gunshot rang out. I called her name, but silence answered me.

December 2000

Her family lived out of town, so I arranged her funeral. In a state of numbness and shock, I chose the coffin, ordered flowers, arranged the music, and even selected her clothes. It was only two weeks before Christmas—not a joyous time for me, to say the least.

On New Year's Eve, I sat alone in my apartment, holding her urn. My tears flowed as I reminisced about the good times we'd had and wondered why it couldn't have turned out differently. Later I would be able to look back on her choices and learn lessons about what not to do. But at the time, all I could do was grieve her loss.

February 2001

January passed and it was a bleak, cold February, unusual for Florida. I should have recognized the chill that blew across my soul–Death was still lingering. It was my dear grandmother. She had fallen. Rushing to the emergency room, where she was taken into surgery, I paced the hallway with my mother and sisters. My grandmother was my best friend. Letting her go would not be easy.

Finally, after three long hours, the doctor came out to inform us that she was doing fine and would probably be able to start physical therapy the next day. But when I saw her, I could see how weak she was. Over the next few weeks, she began to decline. The hospital did everything they could to help her, but she kept insisting she wanted to go "home." So we made arrangements for full-time home care and she was released from the hospital. I went daily to visit her and found her weaker each time.

I'm sure Grandmother knew what was too hard for me to accept—it was just a matter of days and she would be going "home" to be with her husband who had died the year prior. At the end, sitting by her side, I held her hand. I felt angels filling the room, giving me strength. I leaned over and stroked her brow.

"I love you," I whispered. "It's all right for you to go 'home.' I'll be OK."

Moments later she was gone.

My heart was heavy; my friends wondered how much more loss I could take. Thank God I had the support of Dr. Diebel and Mr. Maher, who saw me through the final months approaching my trial.

April 2001

My lawsuit finally settled. Everyone expected me to take a trip and go away for a while, instead I purchased a home and began a remodeling adventure. We all heal at our own pace, and we move through our tough times in different ways. What I needed now was to stay busy. Remodeling is like opening Pandora's box—you never know what you're in for. And I didn't. Every day it seemed like when one fire was put out two more would start up in its place. And the budget I had set in the beginning went out the window about halfway through the project. The most frequent comment I heard was, "Since you've done that, you might at well do this." Thank God my interior designer Mark Rash stepped in to save the day. With a few waves of his hand, the place seemed to magically come together. If I ever realized the value of a professional, it was then.

<u>November 2001</u>

After my home was completed, I was so exhausted from the aftermath, I could do nothing but "veg out" in front of the fireplace with Alex. You can learn a lot about relaxing from cats. Alex would stretch out his furry padded paws across the hardwood floor as he warmed himself by the fireplace. A sight sure to hypnotize anyone. I reminisced with him about how far we had come together. It had been a long road we had been traveling, but now we were in our own home once again and could relax. I even had a secret garden created for him to enjoy. Every now and then I'd catch him warning an occasional drifter cat who had climbed the fence to see what was behind those high walls. It was clear that he was king over his domain.

Alex was not an average cat. Pet lovers understand that
our dear animals are members of our family, with many
human abilities, especially the ability to understand what
we need—unconditional love 24/7. That's what Alex gave
me. We had lived in our new home for six months when
he became ill with kidney disease. Despite everything I
did to save him, his kidneys failed and he died in my
arms. He was an angel to the end, waiting until I was
settled, before he moved on.

Overwhelmed with loss, I felt as if my heart broke
wide open.

I suppose, at this point, most people would snap.
Everyone worried if I would be able to withstand the
agony of so much grief over such a short amount of time.
Some say I threw myself into several projects to distract
me. Whatever I did to numb my pain, my spirit
instinctively knew that I could not stop climbing my
mountain. I had already transitioned from victim to
survivor—and now I was preparing to soar. The fire
within drove me as the yearning and longing of my
dreams strengthened and anchored me.

CHAPTER ELEVEN

My Soul Awakens

Like a phoenix rising from the ashes, my soul was taking flight. I'd never be the same again. My wounded spirit had awakened the fire deep within my soul, forcing me to rise above and learn from all my experiences.

In less than 10 years, I had gone from running a successful business to having a near death experience, to relearning how to walk and talk, enduring a lover's suicide, to losing my beloved grandmother, to overcoming a long and fierce legal battle.

My fiery journey taught me many valuable lessons that would sustain and carry me forward throughout my life. I had reached a simple conclusion during my journey—we are not in control. We can decide how we want to react to our experiences, but only God decides what they will be.

Imagine that we are all pieces in a board game that represents a set of experiences. In the game, there are no winners or losers, but how we choose to manage our moves decides the outcome of our life. We have all been blessed with different gifts and talents, and we all have different challenges to endure, overcome, and learn from. No matter what "game piece" we select, we all have the same opportunity to decide how we use them. Most importantly, we never have the right or responsibility to question or play another person's piece. We can only take care of our own.

All my life, whenever I'd set out to find something, I usually found it or it found me. When I set out to find answers—to find myself, the answers showed up and much quicker than I ever imagined.

I am a big believer of manifesting what you believe is possible. I first learned about manifesting at a personal-growth course. I learned how to ask for what you want and to then prepare for it as if it is coming or has already arrived. Like most everyone, I wanted to experience real love. I had been in love, but it was never quite the right connection. So naturally, I was determined to find it. I had also heard that once you stop looking for love it will come. So I made a little book describing the type of person I would like to spend my life with. When I showed the little red book to my friends they all commented that it might be difficult to find a person possessing all the qualities that I had listed. Nonetheless, I was confident that one day my soul mate and I would find each other.

God must have a sense of humor to be able to watch us work so hard for something that is so easy to receive. Once at summer camp when I was ten, I heard a missionary speak about how simple God made it for us to receive the gift of love. The missionary man stretched out his hand, holding a dollar bill, offering it as a free gift to anyone willing to come receive it. But we sat there, wondering, "What's the catch?" There is none, he explained. It's a free gift; all we had to do was come to receive it. I wish I'd learned then the lesson he tried to teach us that day. I could have saved myself years of therapy.

Unlike giving, receiving requires trust and a sense of worthiness. Without trust we are always questioning the motives and intentions of everything and everyone around us. Imagine if we simply let go of our doubts and fears, trusting that everything is exactly the way it is meant to be, then we would never be unhappy or disappointed with the outcome. We could relax knowing that everything has a purpose.

This concept was finally sinking in. Holding on to the idea that even my stroke had a purpose, I was aware that I had to let go and trust the outcome—that I would find my soul mate.

My life coach shared a simple yet powerful visual for me to focus on whenever I would worry about finding love. She compared searching for love to a fish that swims frantically through the ocean in search of water—it's all around us. In order for me to find the love I felt was hidden, lost, or unattainable, I first had to look within. Once I began looking inward, I began to hear my own inner voice and see myself more clearly.

Holding a sacred space for my life partner, I began taking care of myself and preparing to receive love when it arrived. Shortly after I made this conscious decision, my heart awoke to the undeniable call of love. The instant we met, there was a strong connection. We both experienced an intense, deep love for each other, different from anything we had ever experienced before. It was strongest most karmic feeling I had ever felt. Something very powerful existed between us—we were old soul mates. But, in time our feelings became clouded by our unhealed wounds that were surfacing.

Relationships can bring out the best and the worst in us. I've learned that this is because when we feel safe, cradled in love, our fears and issues begin to surface. We become mirrors of one another's unhealed parts so we can look at them, learn to embrace them, and let them go. I think of relationships as "workshops of life." Some of the finest work we can ever do on ourselves can only be done when we are in a relationship. My biggest issue was the fear of being abandoned. I was so afraid of someone leaving me that I would never really let anyone get too close for fear they might leave. As life would have it, we attract the lessons we need to learn, and those best to experience them with. In other words, we attract what we fear and need to work through.

When you've carried a fear with you for most of your life, it becomes a part of you and is hard to see. But once I saw my fear of abandonment, I couldn't wait to get rid of it. Almost as if I had discovered a leech on my back. Oh my God, get it off!

I accepted the challenge of a separation, believing that whatever the outcome, it would be for the best. With my heart wide open, I gave my partner the space she needed—and I entered into my deepest fear, the fiery furnace I was so sure would burn me up.

The next few weeks were the hardest as I expected my fear to consume me at any time, but to my surprise, it never did. Even though my heart broke when she decided to end our relationship, it was as if I sprang up from a lake, gasping for air. I had not been consumed by the fear of abandonment that I had run from for so long. My experience actually deepened my capacity for love. When she decided that she was not ready for the kind of work a relationship takes, I let her go with love—and without the suffering that I'd always experienced before.

My soul was awakening. I was shifting and growing. It was like my soul had windows and could see. I knew I'd never be the same again, nor would I want to. My old patterns and fears were no longer needed where I was going. Turning to my higher power—the God that had carried me safely through the fire—I surrendered and let go. As the defenses I had built around my heart came crashing down, my life began to change and vibrate at a higher frequency.

I was light and free; my spirit had taken flight. I stopped trying to figure everyone out, understand their actions, or find solutions. I was no longer burdened with being politically correct or concerned with who liked me, who didn't, and why. I could now love without judgments or attachments.

After a long fiery journey, I had discovered the reason for my fate. My stroke was a gift that had forced me to grow and see that the answers I sought were always within me, waiting to be discovered. Love had emptied me out and filled me back up. In my broken state, I had found what was there all along—the fire within my soul.

Looking back I could see all the valuable lessons I had learned from my experiences.

- Having a stroke made me aware of how quickly **life can change.**
- My miraculous recovery showed me that **faith does move mountains.**
- Learning to walk again taught me that **nothing is impossible.**
- The tragic suicide of my lover taught me how important it is to **never give up.**
- Losing loved ones taught me that life does end and to **be with those you love as much as you can.**
- Overcoming a fierce lawsuit taught me that **justice can prevail.**

· My challenges taught me to **let go and trust.**

· And, facing my fear **awakened my soul.**

My tragedies, challenges, and losses changed my life. They forced me to open my eyes, to listen with my heart, and to realize that what really matters is faith, hope, and—most of all—love.

> "Love bears all things;
> believes all things;
> hopes all things;
> and endures all things."

My hope is that you will allow my journey to inspire you to hang on, no matter how tough your battle might be. And to believe that there is a purpose for everything. No matter how high your mountain might seem, start climbing it, one step at a time. You will arrive on the other side before you know it!

I thank God for bringing me to this awareness and sending so many guardian angels to carry me safely through the fire.

Whatever your experience may be, make it count. Life is short. Listen to the message of your heart and find *your* fire within.

Love and courage to you all.

God Bless,

Valerie

If we could untangle the
mysteries of life

and unravel the energies which
run through the world;

if we could evaluate correctly the
significance of passing events;

if we could measure the struggles,
dilemmas, and aspirations of
mankind,

we could find that nothing is
born out of time.

Everything comes at its appointed
moment.

—Joseph R. Sizoo—

EPILOGUE

I now know that my life was altered by a stroke for a reason—it was my destiny. It was God's way of redirecting my life path to an amazing journey filled with faith, compassion, and healing energies. My awareness has expanded, my soul has awakened, and lives have been blessed by my experience.

Because of the expedient response time that has been implemented by the hospital since my stroke, many lives have been saved. We all make mistakes, and we grow when we learn from them. I honor the hospital where my stroke happened for their current expertise in stroke awareness, detection, and treatment.

It moves me deeply to see the faces of my fellow stroke survivors light up when I walk into their hospital room or speak to their group. Looking at me, they realize there is hope. My story has encouraged so many that I've taken a survivor's mission to share the hope and healing I've found.

Every 45 seconds someone in the U.S. has a stroke. Every three minutes, someone dies of a stroke. Stroke is our leading cause of disability and the third leading cause of death, killing more than twice as many women as breast cancer each year. Many of these strokes affect our elders, our parents, and grandparents. But more and more, seemingly healthy young people are affected by stroke. To solve a problem, we must first be aware of it. That is why I devote my time to speaking out about the national epidemic of stroke. My goal is to educate and raise awareness about both the problem of stroke—and its solutions.

If enough of us know the warning signs of stroke and know that it can happen to any of us anywhere, countless lives will be saved. If we see someone in the mall, restaurant, or theater exhibiting signs of stroke, we will know to call 9-1-1. If a friend describes an incident of extreme dizziness or slurred speech for no reason, we'll know enough to warn them to get to the closest ER.

And if enough of us hold a collective intention to find solutions to stroke, then new, effective prevention and treatment options will become available. Many powerful methods to prevent and treat stroke have already been developed and are being used in other countries—but are not yet obtainable here. That must change. Will you join me in working toward that change? Check my Web site for resources and ways to get involved. Thank you.

www.thefirewithin.net

Photo: Dennis Dean Images

These are some of the key warning signs of a stroke that my fellow survivors and I want you to know:

- Sudden numbness or weakness on one side of your face, arm, or leg

- Sudden slurred speech

- Extreme dizziness and nauseousness

- Sudden blurred vision

- Trouble with balance and coordination, difficulty walking

- Sudden severe headache

NOT ALL THESE WARNING SIGNS OCCUR IN EVERY STROKE. IF SOME OCCUR, DON'T WAIT—GET HELP IMMEDIATELY! EVERY SECOND COUNTS! STROKE IS A MEDICAL EMERGENCY. CALL 9-1-1.

GLOSSARY OF TERMS

Multiple sclerosis is thought to be an autoimmune disease of the central nervous system in which gradual destruction of myelin occurs in patches throughout the brain or spinal cord or both, causing muscular weakness, loss of coordination, and speech or visual disturbances.

CT Scan uses advanced X-ray technology to see inside the brain, into areas that cannot be seen on regular X rays.

MRI, or Magnetic Resonance Imaging, uses pulsing radio waves to create intricately detailed 2D or 3D images. An incredibly accurate diagnostic tool, it requires a patient to lie on a pallet which is inserted into the closed, tunnel-like device. The patient must lie completely still for 20 to 90 minutes, and must tolerate a tremendous amount of noise (a continual, rapid hammering sound).

Inderal is the brand name for the drug *Propranolol,* a beta blocker, used to dilate the blood vessels, to reduce constriction associated with migraines.

Vertigo is an illusion of motion with a distinct sensation of rotation; acute dizziness. Persons affected find it difficult to maintain upright posture.

Meclizine is the generic name for the drug most often used to treat vertigo.

Coumadin is the brand name for the drug *warfarin,* which is an anticoagulant, or blood thinner.

Plavix is the brand name for the drug *clopidogrel,* which prevents platelets (substances in the blood) from clustering, helping to keep the blood from forming clots.

ThickenUp is an instant thickening product made by Novartis which is used to help prevent aspiration.

Reflexology is a natural healing art, based on the principle that there are reflexes in the feet and hands which correspond to every part of the body. By stimulating and applying pressure to the feet or hands, you are increasing circulation and promoting specific bodily and muscular functions.

Hospital of the Americas was a clinic in Puerto Plata, Dominican Republic. It no longer exists.

Live stem cell injections replace diseased or dysfunctional cells with healthy functioning ones. Stem cells are precursor cells that can give rise to multiple tissue type cells and are injected into the body. There are many types of stem cells which are being researched to treat cancers, Parkinson's disease, spinal-cord injuries, heart disease, and diabetes.

Hyperbaric oxygen treatments, originally developed to treat scuba divers with the bends, is now being used for many medical conditions. The entire body is placed under increased atmospheric pressure in a closely monitored airtight chamber. During HBO therapy, the patient breathes 100% oxygen, delivering additional oxygen to the body tissues.

Chelation IV is an intravenous solution containing chelating agents which bind to the toxic metals in the body, and carry them to the kidneys or colon to be excreted.

Acupressure is an ancient Chinese technique (based on acupuncture, but using finger pressure and not needles) to access and release blocked or congested energy in the body.

Color-laser therapy aids in tissue healing and cell regeneration by stimulating the cell photoreceptors to absorb laser energy.

Colonics, or colon hydrotherapy, removes toxic debris from
  the colon by circulating a gentle flow of filtered,
  temperature-controlled water, coaxing out impurities.

Ionized oxygen therapy is widely used in Europe to improve
  microcirculation, regulate pH values, and reduce pain
  and inflammation. Medical grade oxygen is ionized by
  adding either a positive or negative charge, and can
  then be inhaled or mixed with medications.

Valerian is an herb used for its calming properties.

Fibromyalgia is a disorder that results in chronic and often
  acute musculoskeletal pain and fatigue, similar to a
  bad flu. It affects people of all ages, and its cause is
  not yet known.